Singles PLUS

THE BIBLE AND BEING SINGLE

Ray Mossholder

Creation House
Lake Mary, Florida

Creation House
Strang Communications Company
190 North Westmonte Drive
Altamonte Springs, FL 32714
(407) 862-7565

First printing, July 1991
Second printing, June 1992
Third printing, December 1992
Fourth printing, June 1993

*To my darlin' Arlyne
and our two very happy Christ-centered singles:
Bethany and David Mossholder.*

*To two happily married couples:
our own son and his wife,
Tim and Kelly Mossholder,
and our "spiritual son" and his wife,
Larry and Reneé Jack.
These couples are happily married
because they followed Christ so closely
in their dating lives and still follow Him.*

*To the two single "spiritual daughters"
who grew in Christ within our home:
Dorothy Hedlund and Celia Shrago.*

*To another of our "spiritual daughters" and
our choice for "Best Single Parent of This Generation":
Diane Brackin.*

*We love you and greatly rejoice
over what Jesus Christ is doing in your lives.*

ACKNOWLEDGMENTS

The great news is, "For God so loved the world, that He gave His only begotten [*single*] Son" (John 3:16). God did that so you and I could choose to receive Jesus Christ as Lord and have eternal life in heaven rather than in hell (John 3:17-21). Christ came to earth and stayed unmarried throughout His lifetime.

Oh, He did get *engaged*. One day I'll celebrate at His wedding dinner with *all* who "come to the light" (John 3:20). I hope you'll be there. May this book help you better understand His love letter to you — the Bible. Lord God, thanks for proposing to us. As for me, I respond: I do.

Many bouquets of American beauty roses to my darlin' Arlyne, my wife and extremely personal secretary. While I've been writing this book, she's been painting our kitchen. Talk about patience! Her encouragement, prayers and faith in God and me are a constant inspiration. She makes me understand why so many singles want to get married. The deep regret of my life is the time each year we have to live as if single, away from each other. (My traveling ministry makes this necessary.) God gives us the strength to endure, as He will every single person who follows Christ.

More praise to God for Oral Roberts University and Regent University (CBN) graduate Kirk Mitchell — "Tonto" for this "Lone Ranger." Where would I be without him as my executive travel assistant? To give you an idea of his importance, I hit a wrong button while writing this book; an entire chapter disappeared, lost in the dark sea of computer no-man's land. Though I thought it was lost forever, Kirk got it back. I fear Kirk will have phone marks on one ear for the rest of his life — evidence of all the calling he's done on this book's behalf. Readers, you may thank him for the questions at the end of each chapter. (And he's single, too.)

Thanks to my son David for his outstanding research for this book. His extensive reading on the topic and gleaning of quotes have been a huge help to me. Now he's doing research for all his homework at Oral Roberts University.

Praise God for Sam and Paulette Farina, who, along with people from Christian Assembly in Columbus, Ohio, lovingly gave me a new laptop computer. It's *so* fast! Their church is great!

Another thanks to Dorothy Hedlund and her keen-eyed initial editing of *Singles Plus*

More bouquets to Evelyn Bence and Debbie Cole. Their brilliant editing of my first book, *Marriage Plus*, and now this one makes me hope they'll work on all my books. Debbie is a sheer delight and gifted at dotting every "i" and crossing every "t." I look forward to every conversation with her, because I learn so much. Thanks, too, to my warmhearted publisher, Murray Fisher. And to Jerry Parsons and Mark Poulalion, who deeply care about ministering to people through Creation House — a great company. With Steve Strang at the head of it, how could it be anything else?

A round of applause to president Wes Wilson and my Marriage Plus ministry board: Jon Cook, John Zachman, Rev. Jack Duitsman, Max Lile and Rob Buchheit — men who keep me on the straight and narrow.

A holy hug to my extremely gifted office manager, Deanna Parris, and another to my very creative seminar director, Ed Snyder.

A doff of my hat (which uncovers a bald head) to Jerry D. Jones and his outstanding staff of the *Single Adult Ministries Journal.* I don't know how anyone working with singles can keep up with pertinent ideas, resources and information without subscribing to this journal.

As for the humor in this book, for more than twenty years I've collected every joke that has made me laugh — from newspapers, magazines, television and so forth. It's impossible to credit all my humor sources. If you want to start a collection of your own, buy all the joke books compiled by Bob Phillips (Harvest House and Zondervan), E.C. McKenzie (Baker Books), Croft M. Pentz (Tyndale House) and my hilarious friend Vern McClellan (Harvest House, Tyndale House and Here's Life).

Last but far from least, hallelujah to God for the donors who are the lifeblood of both Marriage Plus and Singles Plus. No church or organization sponsors these ministries. They exist because God prompts people to give. Thanks to all those who respond to Him. This book exists because of them.

*"Thy word I have treasured in my heart,
That I may not sin against Thee."*
Psalm 119:11

*"The one who obeys Me
is the one who loves Me;
and because he (or she) loves Me,
My Father will love him (or her);
and I will too,
and I will reveal Myself to him (or her).
Jesus replied, 'Because I will only reveal Myself
to those who love Me and obey Me.
The Father will love them too,
and we will come to them
and live with them.' "*
John 14:21,23, LB

*"Stay always within
the boundaries where God's love
can reach and bless you."*
Jude 21a, LB

CONTENTS

This book is freeing. I love the principles in it. While reading I was reminded of how wonderfully powerful it is to be single and how wonderfully powerful it is to be married — when we are wonderfully empowered by the Lord.

I would give this book to those singles who are "seeking" a mate so that any misspent energies would come under the control of the Word, and also to those singles who are content — to reaffirm and support their completeness in being single.

I loved the attitude and humor that Ray displayed in this book. Above all I come back again and again to the realization that, if our partnership with Christ isn't solid and first, nothing in our lives will be complete.

A good encouraging book for anyone.

Annie Herring
formerly of the Second Chapter of Acts

It is no secret that society has undergone radical and abrupt changes during the past twenty-plus years. No change has perhaps been as unexpected and unaddressed as the ever-increasing phenomenon of single adulthood. Singles will soon represent more than 50 percent of all the adult population in America. We are no longer a nation of "Leave It to Beaver" or "Ozzie and Harriet" families. Today's landscape is made up of a growing group of blended families and single adults (never married, divorced, widowed, single parents).

Since we are charged by Jesus Christ to impact society (Matt. 5:13-16) and not to be shaped by it (Rom. 12:1-2), we would be wise to acknowledge society's changes, adjust our approach with readiness and understanding (1 Pet. 3:15) and never compromise the one sure thing we have: the truth of the gospel.

We must seek to minister to the challenges facing singles that are ultimately common to the human condition. As a singles' pastor I am especially committed to ministering God's Word, love and power to singles.

Here are three biblical truths of special significance for singles:

The value of everyone (Ps. 139:13-16): God repeatedly acknowledges the worth of each individual. We would be most prudent to consider the intentional variety of members God has established in His body, work to see each person free to fulfill his or her gift and calling and provide, as best we can, the necessary support. These challenges are demanding, yet Jesus has assured us of success if we will follow His way.

The value of increased opportunity (1 Cor. 7:32-35): A single adult has the unique opportunity for total devotion to the Lord. To this one adds practical service. Taking the gifts, talents and skills God has bestowed and using them for His glory are among the most rewarding aspects of living.

Worth is not devalued by need (Matt. 9:10-13; 1 Cor. 1:26-29): Often the needs of single adults are as great as those of married persons. Where need exists let ministry empowered by the Holy Spirit take place. Where health is apparent, acknowledge and affirm the individual as a righteous model for others to emulate within the kingdom of God.

Societal changes will continue at an accelerating pace. But some things will never change. Practical biblical truths will always provide the liberty and security each individual seeks. You will find an abundance within the covers of this book.

John Tolle
Director of Single Adult Ministries
The Church on the Way
Van Nuys; California
July 1991

Dear Ray,

I'm a Christian, and I've met the greatest guy in the world. We met at a bar. (I don't usually frequent such places, but I was there with a friend.) Jim and I talked all evening. We've been inseparable ever since (about six months). He's a Christian but doesn't go to church. Because he's not a churchgoer, my mom and dad have been against him from the start.

Now Jim has asked me to marry him, and my folks are having a cow. I think I love Jim. True, he swears some, smokes and drinks a little, and (in my dad's words) "can't keep a job." But he loves me, and if we don't get married soon I'm afraid, as passionate as he is, I'm going to end up having sex with him. I don't want to do that and violate God's will. How can I convince my folks Jim and I should get married?

Loved by Jim

*Unless the Lord builds
the house, they labor
in vain who build it.*

Psalm 127:1

GETTING THE RIGHT START

Marriage is too often a case where
cupidity meets stupidity.

A week before I met my darlin' Arlyne I wrote a brilliant statement in my diary. Judge it for yourself: "If all the lonely people in the world would just get together...no one would ever be lonely again!"

Only after we got married would I realize how wrong my "brilliant statement" really was. The truth is, if all the lonely people in the world got together, there would simply be a lot of lonely people together.

I married Arlyne, and after the first few episodes of sex were over (within about two weeks), I wanted a divorce. I stuck it out until one day, ten years later, when

I sat on the top stair in front of our second-story apartment in San Bruno, California, waiting for our oldest son, Tim, to come home from kindergarten. I had to tell him something. My car was already packed; I was leaving.

When he spotted me, he threw out his arms to give me a big hug. "Daddy!" He ran up the steps as excited as a little boy can be.

I hugged him tightly and then blurted out, "Son, Daddy is going away. I'm not going to live at your house anymore. I'm sorry, and I'll really miss you."

Suddenly I felt his racking sobs. He clung to me as if he'd never let me go. God and my little boy had gotten through my thick skull. Even though I'd try again later, I couldn't leave. They had my heart.

It may surprise you to know I was a Christian when this incident took place. I knew the Lord. I even "loved" the Lord. In fact, my love for the Lord (and not my love for my wife) kept me in my marriage into the twelfth year. During that twelfth year I began to discover what God meant when He said in Isaiah 55:8-9:

> "For My thoughts are not your thoughts,
> Neither are your ways My ways," declares the Lord.
> "For as the heavens are higher than the earth,
> So are My ways higher than your ways,
> And My thoughts than your thoughts."

While at a two-month Youth With a Mission conference in Switzerland, I devoured my Bible. Miserable in my marriage, I spent night after night, all alone, poring over every scripture I could find on every aspect of married life. God gave me the answers to every question I asked Him. The result was not only the extreme blessing of my own marriage, but the birth of the Marriage Plus seminar I teach.

A few years ago that same boy who threw himself into my lap, now grown and a youth pastor at a Southern California church, asked if I would undertake the same kind of Bible study regarding the single life so I could teach the singles at his church. The result of his challenge was the birth of the Singles Plus seminar.

Every unmarried person needs to understand what I hadn't understood when I wrote my "profound" statement about loneliness. *The only thing worse than being SINGLE and lonely is being MARRIED and lonely!*

The purpose of this book is not to talk you out of — or into — marriage. When Jesus Christ becomes the center of any marriage, life can be beautiful. But in America there are now:

- One divorce in every two marriages
- Two divorces out of every five first marriages
- One divorce in every three Protestant marriages

- One divorce in every four Roman Catholic marriages

I don't cite these statistics to discourage you. If I had seen these truths about divorce while I was still single, I would have said, "That won't happen to me!" (And by God's grace it hasn't.) But today I would go further than these statistics. I would say maybe one in five of the marriages that don't end in divorce are truly happy marriages. Most marriages, once the honeymoon is over, range in levels from being warring to boring to snoring! Yet marriage doesn't have to be like that. God created the whole idea of marriage, and He designed it to work.

God's Amazing Guidebook

Puzzled over a final exam question, one college student finally wrote, "Only God knows the answer to this question. Merry Christmas." He received the graded paper back: "God gets an A. You get an F. Happy New Year!"

Yes, God knows the answers to *everything*. The Bible is not *an* amazing book. The Bible is *the* amazing book that has survived the ignorance of its friends and the hatred of its enemies.

Australian pastor Phil Pringle reminds us:

> The man who delights in the Word of God and meditates in it day and night "will be like a tree planted by the rivers of water. His leaf will not wither. He will bring forth fruit in its season. And whatever He does will prosper" (Ps. 1:2-3). When we have no room for the Word of God in our lives we have no room for success. Many different situations come into our world. Some good, some bad. No matter what happens, however, we are called by God to fix our attention upon the Word.
>
> There is a marked difference between the truth and the facts. People are very quick to let us know what the "facts" are. However, our faith, focus and fight are based on the truth, not the facts. God's Word stands high in opposition to many of the situations we face. We are to make the choice. We believe God's Word, or we believe "the facts." If we are to enjoy the great blessing of God, we need to choose the truth every time. It may contradict the circumstance. Often it will.
>
> Peter told Jesus that they had fished all night and still "caught nothing. Nevertheless at thy word we will let down the nets for a catch" (Luke 5:5). How is a carpenter going to tell an experienced fisherman how to fish? But Peter recognized this was no mere carpenter. This was the Word of God. He chose the truth over the facts. The facts of experience and knowledge said there were no fish out there. The Truth

said, "There are, so get out there and haul them in!" Truth versus facts.

Joshua was told that when he meditated in the Word of God (Josh. 1:8) he would also have success. This is something we must have. For God and for ourselves. The alternative is horrifying.[1]

God is not interested only in redeeming a person's soul; He is interested in making a person whole: body, soul and spirit. Single or married, people will find the "abundant life" (John 10:10) only by following God's rules, as recorded in the Bible.

Acting on the Rules

Some people don't like rules, or they believe rules are made to be broken; rules (especially God's) interfere too much with fun. But people who want their marriages to be the best God designed them to be must follow the rules He has set. As Proverbs 29:18 (KJV) warns, "Where there is no vision, the people perish." The word *vision* means "goals," which require a set of guidelines. Think of the "perished" marriages among your own friends and family. Ask those involved how many biblical guidelines they followed in preparing for marriage, and you'll see just how true Proverbs 29:18 is. Good marriages seldom just happen but rather result from following God's plans before marriage (or, as in my case, discovering them afterward, which is the painful route to take).

> Therefore everyone who *hears these words of Mine, and acts upon them*, may be compared to a wise man, who built his house upon the rock. And the rain descended, and the floods came, and the winds blew, and burst against that house; and yet it did not fall, for it had been founded upon the rock. And everyone who *hears these words of Mine, and does not act upon them*, will be like a foolish man, who built his house upon the sand. And the rain descended, and the floods came, and the winds blew, and burst against that house; and it fell, and great was its fall (Matt. 7:24-27, italics mine).

Ever consider breaking the law of gravity? I did hear about one optimist who tried it by jumping off the Empire State Building. As the story goes, while falling past the fifth floor, he said, "Well, so far, so good!"

Like gravity, God's laws last longer than those who break them.

When the devil first tempted Eve, he didn't try to get her to hate God or murder Adam. He suggested she take her life into her own hands and out of God's control. Then Adam — sold on slick serpent salesmanship — found being self-centered

20

instead of God-centered a delicious experience. By the time the eyes of Adam and Eve were opened to what they'd done (Gen. 3:1-7), they had destroyed their world. How much are you tempted to take your life into your own hands? How often do you find yourself self-centered instead of God-centered? How willing are you to follow Christ so that your world isn't destroyed?

You don't break the law of gravity; it breaks you. In the very same way, you don't break the natural laws or rules God has set concerning marriage or the single life. If you break those rules, they will break you.

Defining Terms

Since this book will have a great deal to say about singles and the choices they have about marriage, let's define our terms. *Single* adults are those widowed, divorced or never married.

What is *Christian* marriage? The world is working hard to change all the definitions of marriage. But God's Word never changes, and a Christian marriage must be sealed by a legal document (a covenant) recognized by both God and the government (Titus 3:1), carrying a lifetime guarantee. The two persons entering into the contract must be one single Christian male and one single Christian female who have chosen each other and are legally qualified to marry. Any other kind of arrangement, though it may be a marriage in every legal way and binding by law, disqualifies the marriage from being a *Christian* marriage — in which both persons were already Christians before they married each other.

It is true that a husband or wife can be saved after he or she is already into a marriage. But the heartache and trauma suffered in experiencing marriage with a lost spouse is something to be avoided at all costs. Ask my wife!

Surrendering to Christ

A friend recently told me of someone who could "lie good." In other words, he could "talk a good line" while being totally insincere. In the same way, many people try to claim they're Christians when they don't live the Christian life. They lie good.

In his book *I Surrender: Submitting to Christ in the Details of Life*, Patrick W. Morley writes:

> The partially surrendered life may be Christian in spirit, but it is secular in practice.... We must learn how to surrender to Christ in the details of daily life. Over the past few decades, many of us started off on the wrong foot with Jesus Christ. It is the proposition that Jesus can be

Savior without being *Lord*. It is the idea that one can *add* Christ, but not *subtract* sin. Many of us have merely added Christ to our lives as another interest in an already busy and otherwise overcrowded schedule. This sort of thinking has watered down the meaning of a personal relationship with Christ.... Many men and women I have met express complete, utter frustration about leading the kind of defeated (sometimes counterfeit), partially surrendered life — the life of a cultural Christian.... But the Bible calls men and women to a *turning point*, to a radical, life-transforming change. This turning point is no mean challenge, but a full surrender to history's most ideal, most radical leader: the Lord Jesus Christ.[2]

If 33 percent of all adult Americans claim to be evangelical or born-again Christians, why has our country's moral fiber gone down the tubes? Because we're a nation of good liars — claiming faith without works. James 2:17 says that faith without corresponding works is dead. James went on to say that even the demons believe in God — and shudder (v. 19). "Good liars" often aren't even smart enough to shudder.

The Love of God and the Blessings of God

The greatest biblical truth anyone will ever share with you is this: God loves you (John 3:16; Rom. 5:8-9; Eph. 2:4-7). It doesn't matter if you've just robbed a blind man or murdered your mother, God still loves you. In fact, nothing you could ever do would stop God from loving you (Rom. 8:38-39).

The *love* of God is *unconditional*, but the continuous *blessings* of God are totally *conditional* (Matt. 6:14-15; 7:24-27; John 8:31-32; Rom. 8:9,17; Col. 1:21-23; 1 John 5:1-5). Just as it matters which way you point the nose of a rocket if you want that rocket to hit the moon, so too it matters whether or not you follow God's biblical directions. You'll be blessed *only* if you do — blessed in your singleness or in your marriage.

Millions of people make a private hell for themselves here on earth and will be in hell forever because they refuse to give their lives to Jesus Christ — in truth — and follow God's directions in His Word (Matt. 7:21-27; John 3:16-21; Rom. 1:18-32; 6:16; Heb. 3:12-4:2; 2 Pet. 2:1-22). Meanwhile, millions find the blessings of love, joy, peace (Gal. 5:22-23) and abundant life because they *do* obey Christ (John 14:15) and act upon God's Word (Matt. 7:24-25). Which way are you headed right now?

Maybe you've never asked Jesus Christ to transform your life. Or you may have begun a walk with Christ, then made poor choices that have led you away from

Him. Maybe you've been "too busy" to stay in the Bible; maybe you've never understood that it is the only book that lays out the directions for abundant life. If any of these things apply to you, read this carefully:

> If we say that we have fellowship with Him and yet walk in the darkness, we lie and do not practice the truth; but if we walk in the light as He Himself is in the light, we have fellowship with one another, and the blood of Jesus Christ His Son cleanses us from all sin. If we say that we have no sin, we are deceiving ourselves, and the truth is not in us. If we confess our sins, He is faithful and righteous to forgive us our sins and to cleanse us from all unrighteousness (1 John 1:6-9).

If you've been doing your own thing rather than following Christ, confess your sins. Like the prodigal son's father (Luke 15:11-32), your heavenly Father will forgive you and restore you to His royalty. The Greek word translated "confess" literally means "to say the same thing as." God calls sin *sin*, and He asks that you do the same. Yet confession without a change of ways isn't enough. Let God give you the power to *stop* your sin. After asking Him to do that, change your ways. Follow God's directions in His Word, and don't return to your sin.

If you've never asked Jesus Christ to forgive your sins and become your Lord, do it now. Here's how:

> "The Word is near you, in your mouth and in your heart" — that is, the word of faith which we are preaching, that if you confess with your mouth Jesus as Lord, and believe in your heart that God raised Him from the dead, you shall be saved; for with the heart man [woman, boy or girl] believes, resulting in righteousness, and with the mouth he confesses, resulting in salvation (Rom. 10:8-10).

You might pray these very words: Dear Lord Jesus Christ, forgive my sins. I want to know You. I want to follow You. Be my Savior and my Lord. I'll read Your Word. I'll believe Your Word. I'll do what Your Word says. Thank You for saving me and for giving me the power to follow You. You alone give eternal life. I'll follow You forever, Lord. Amen.

If you prayed this prayer sincerely, the Holy Spirit has come inside your spirit.

Because Jesus Christ died on the cross in your place (Rom. 5:8-11) to cancel your sins (Is. 53:3-5; Col. 1:19-23), He is your Savior (Titus 3:5-7) as well as your Lord (Matt. 7:21). Christ and you are an unbeatable combination and can defeat all of the devil's plans for you. You are never alone when you are walking and working with Jesus Christ (Heb. 13:5; 2 Cor. 6:1).

Rejoice! You are totally new (2 Cor. 5:17), born again (John 3:3). All your previous sins are washed away in the blood of Christ, and He has given you the power to resist sin from now on (1 John 5:5-6). You haven't reached perfection, but you have God's power available to reject sin. Use it. As you continue to grow in your walk with Christ, pray what David prayed in Psalm 19:12: "Clear me from hidden [and unconscious] faults" (Amplified). From time to time, when God knows you're ready, He'll let you recognize hidden faults and show you how to overcome them. Try to please God from now on in everything you do or say; as you study the Bible daily, it will keep you informed on what pleases Him.

As far as your past goes, God can use anything to bring glory to Himself (Rom. 8:28). And as far as your future goes, God is already there while He's working with you here and now!

Now tell another person that you've asked Jesus Christ to be Lord of your life (Rom. 10:9). I invite you to call my office and tell one of my staff. We will pray with you and answer your questions. Our office hours are 9:00 a.m. to 5:00 p.m. (Pacific Time), weekdays; telephone: (818) 882-9424.

Someone has said, "A Bible that is falling apart usually belongs to someone who isn't." Whether you have just become a Christian or are right now returning to your walk with Christ, *spend time in the Bible daily* (1 Pet. 2:2). Choose a version you can understand. Begin by studying one of the Gospels (Matthew, Mark, Luke or John). The Bible can easily be read through in seventy hours. Set aside a realistic amount of time each day or night, reading the New Testament first. Then read through the entire Bible. Studying the Bible daily will help you grow in your faith for the rest of your life (2 Tim. 2:15; 3:16-17).

One handy study Bible I recommend is *The One Year Bible* (Tyndale House), available in several different translations. If you don't read the Bible through in seventy hours, at least you can do it with this Bible in one year.

Pray anytime, anywhere (1 Thess. 5:17). Develop a daily time of prayer, and talk to God about anything. After talking with Him, be still for several minutes and listen. He will often have something important to say to you. A great book to help you understand prayer is *Prayer Is Invading the Impossible* (Ballentine) by my pastor, Jack Hayford.

Most people miss church services becasue they live too far from God, not because they live too far from the building! *If you are not already in a Christ-centered, Bible-believing church, find one and join it* (Heb. 10:23-25; Eph. 4:11-16). The pastor will be able to help you grow as a Christian, teaching you God's directions for the Christian life and showing you how to help others find and grow in Christ.

Why I Wrote This Book

"How can an old married geezer like you teach us singles anything?"

The young man who asked me that question wasn't trying to be rude. My bald head and wedding ring were simply giant barriers to him.

He needed answers for the single life. I'm not single. I've been married more than half my life. And as for my age, "A gray head is a crown of glory" (Prov. 16:31), but I've yet to figure out what my bald head represents!

So what are my credentials?

1. *I have a memory — oh, what a memory!* As a single guy of twenty-two, I kept a diary. I remember the dating, the waiting and the deep desire for mating.

Yet it wasn't all bad. Being single provides a freedom to make choices that no godly married person can ever know. As I've written in my book *Marriage Plus*,

> You both gain and lose when you get married. You gain a partner who will work with you (if you're marrying a Christian) and help you be more than you could ever be without that person. But you lose the ability to do everything on your own, do only what you want to do, eat only what you want to eat, sleep in if you don't want to get up, watch only the TV programs you want to see, quit a job if you don't like it, move to another town if you prefer, or join the circus. In short, you lose the ability to be selfish without paying a horrible price.[3]

Quite frankly, I remember liking that kind of freedom.

2. *I tried to live single even after I was married!* I wasn't a Christian when I married Arlyne (though I thought I was). Seven years into my marriage, when I became a rock 'n' roll disc jockey in the San Francisco Bay area, I found that acting single made me more popular with the girls. Why not pretend? I figured. I know the total stupidity of that game.

3. *With the traveling for ministry that I do without my wife, both of us have to live "single" many weeks of the year.* I know what it is to be alone and aching for my wife. I know the emptiness of hotel or motel rooms. The television set is always ready to offer me sexual fantasy. The bar is downstairs. Temptation doesn't die when a person gets married. Even when married couples are together every day, anything — from moods to spats — can make them feel lonely.

4. *I've counseled thousands of married couples.* Many are headed for divorce (and God heads them off at the pass). Even more are "emotionally divorced," determined to stay in their marriages with gritted teeth. But I also meet many Christians who have beautiful marriages and come to the seminars just to learn more. I ask each couple, good marriage or bad, about their premarriage attitudes

and actions. What decisions led to their marriage (or marriages)? The more seminars I conduct, the more clearly certain patterns emerge. What people think and do as singles influences the success or failure of their marriages.

5. *My teaching is grounded in God's Word.* Psalm 127:1 states, "Unless the Lord builds the house, they labor in vain who build it." That's precisely why this book is being written: to share God's Word about the single life, dating, courtship and the possibility of marriage.

Recently Arlyne and I had a new roof put on our home. It was one quick job — complete in two days. But suppose we'd needed a foundation for our house, not a roof. How long would *that* have taken? Far too many couples move into marriage without establishing a proper foundation. Millions of other singles stay single, believing marriage can't possibly work. But with Christ it *can.*

This book is based on some of the lectures presented during the Singles Plus seminars, and it will minister to all ages. It was written to help you understand the biblical foundations that must undergird your life — whether or not you ever marry.

Happy reading!

**Single or married, life's
greatest tragedy is to lose God and never
miss Him until it's too late.**

Questions for Reflection and Discussion

1. Discuss the statement "The only thing worse than being single and lonely is being married and lonely." Can singles involved in close relationships with friends and family still experience deep loneliness? Is marriage a cure for loneliness? Why or why not?

2. Many singles do not have a vision or goals for their life. Often this is because of apathy over relationships with other people; that is, not caring about anything because they feel that other people may not care about them. What does Proverbs 29:18 have to say about those who have no "progressive vision"? How can putting Christ first, following His ways and growing in a relationship with Him help you have a vision for your life? How will having a clear vision for your life make you more content in your single life and a better candidate for a stable marriage? Write down your answers.

3. Many singles feel that God doesn't really know or understand them. Carefully read Jeremiah 29:11 and Psalm 139:13-16. What do these verses say to you about God's intimate knowledge of you *as an individual* and His perfect plan for *you*? Now read Hebrews 4:14-15. Can Jesus really understand the struggles you are going through? According to Hebrews 4:16, how should you approach God even during moments of weakness in your life? Why does the flesh *not* want to do this? (Meditate on Col. 2:6-7, LB.)

4. Many Christians, single and married, try to live the Christian life with one foot still in the world. They believe in Christ, but their behavior does not reflect that the fruit of the Spirit is present. (See Gal. 5:19-23 for the contrast.) They often conclude that the Christian life does not work because they aren't receiving the blessings of God or seeing the promises of God fulfilled in their lives. Can someone who has not totally surrendered his life to Christ receive the blessings of God according to James 1:7-8? Is surrendering to Christ a process, or does it happen instantaneously?

5. When you are trying to get to know someone, is there any substitute for spending *quality* time with them? How can spending quality time with the Lord help you become better prepared for the trials and tribulations that will come your way as a single Christian (James 1:2-4)? Find at least five verses in the Bible that illustrate the desire of the Lord for you to fellowship with Him and thus grow stronger. Write these verses down and keep them where you'll see them often.

Dear Ray,

I'm going to be very honest with you. I'm in a panic. All of my close friends are married. I'm not. I'm a thirty-two-year-old secretary and have wanted to be married since I was seventeen. I have read the Yale-Harvard study on singles and know my chances for marriage seem less than the chances I'll be eaten by a giraffe. What am I to do with the rest of my life? How am I ever going to enjoy growing old alone? Since all the guys in my age-range are taken now, shall I marry a Cub Scout or some old man or just die a lonely old maid?

Over the Hill at Thirty-two

We are not all the same.
God gives some the gift
of a husband or wife,
and others he gives the gift
of being able to stay
happily unmarried.
1 Corinthians 7:7b, LB

ONE

THE GIFT OF BEING SINGLE

*Any roomful of married people is empty
because there isn't a single person in it.*

D oes this scenario sound familiar?
"I went through the Twenty-Two-Year-Old Panic...when I wondered if I were doomed to Old Maidhood (fate worse than death!) because I did not receive my Mrs. degree concurrently with my B.A. I went through the Twenty-Five-Year-Old Panic, searching in the mirror for horrid age spots and dating Attila the Hun for the chance to get out of the library. My *mother* went through the Twenty-Seven-Year-Old Panic for me — I had other responsibilities on my mind at the time.... In the years between twenty and thirty, I was engaged

once, 'almost' engaged a second time, in love with several men, and a bridesmaid to most of my friends."[1]

The author, Penelope Stokes, expresses the concern — even panic — I hear from singles time and again. Why me? God, give me a mate! Get me off this track!

Single adults often look forward to marriage as if their lives will start on that future day. *That's when I'll gain companionship, a partner, an identity, a home. Life in the present tense couldn't possibly be God's will for me.*

John Fischer and Lia Fuller O'Neill's book *Single Person's Identity* is one of the best I've read on the single life. They also describe the holding pattern of many singles:

> The suggestion creeps into the back of my mind that I'm incomplete. I'm in a holding pattern. I'm flying around trying to find the airport so that I can get my feet on the ground and start living. This type of thinking keeps me from living *now*, to be what God has called me to be. It can be very subtle. It comes up in the way I live around the house, and the way I keep my room. I keep thinking..."when"...*"when"* I have my own place...or *"when"* I have someone with me, *then* I'll do this or that.[2]

But in her excellent article, Penelope Stokes goes on to explain a change that occurred in her thinking:

> Somewhere in my twenty-ninth year, I began to realize that singleness, too, is the gift of God. He promised to meet my needs — not in martyrdom, as I "abandoned all hope of marriage and cast myself upon Him," but in the gracious, loving, all-fulfilling way that He meets the other needs of my life — step by trusting step.[3]

What? Singleness as a gift of God? Yes, His Word makes it clear. The apostle Paul wrote:

> I'm not saying you *must* marry; but you certainly *may* if you wish. I wish everyone could get along without marrying, just as I do. But we are not all the same. God gives some the gift of a husband or wife, and others he gives the gift of being able to stay happily unmarried. So I say to those who aren't married, and to widows — better to stay unmarried if you can, just as I am (1 Cor. 7:6-8, LB).

A good look at the Bible shows the value of the single life.

During every Singles Plus seminar I ask everyone to shout out the names of all the happily married couples in the New Testament. The result of this game shocks nearly everybody. After naming Joseph and Mary (Matt. 1:18ff.), Zacharias and Elizabeth (Luke 1:5ff.), Peter (1 Cor. 9:5), Philip (Acts 21:8-9), and Priscilla and Aquila (Acts 18:1-3), they stop. I mean, who wants to mention the only other famous married couple of the New Testament: Ananias and Sapphira (Acts 5:1-10)?!

True, the Old Testament does name many more married couples, but nearly all those marriage relationships were dysfunctional, many polygamous.

Now name every prominent single person who was a leader during New Testament times. Beginning with Jesus Christ, the list may include every writer of the New Testament except Peter. And then there are Timothy, Barnabas, Titus, Philemon, Onesimus, Epaphras, John the Baptist.... If any of these people were married, the Bible is silent about it.

Isn't it strange that churches often want to consider only married pastors? Some have rules that stop singles from being elders. That means Jesus Christ couldn't have been an elder in their church! Granted, I've seen many married couples doing a powerful job of serving God together. But I've seen singles in the same places doing an equally powerful job.

The idea that only married people are fully mature is not only unbiblical but ungodly. Was Jesus mature? You'd better believe He was (Luke 2:52; John 14:6). And so were the single leaders of the early church.

Has it dawned on you that if you love Jesus Christ, are honestly trying to follow Him and are single, it's because that is God's will for you right now? (If you are single and someone is near you, look up from this book and tell that person, "I'm single this minute because I'm totally committed to God's will for my life.")

A Closer Look at the Gift

In 1 Corinthians 7:7 Paul referred to the gift of being single. Jesus indicated the same thing. Answering the disciples' question — Is it better not to marry? — Jesus said:

> Not all men can accept this statement, but only those to whom it has been *given*. For there are eunuchs who were born that way from their mother's womb; and there are eunuchs who were made eunuchs by men; and there are also eunuchs who made themselves eunuchs for the sake of the kingdom of heaven. He who is able to accept this, let him accept it (Matt. 19:11-12, italics mine).

Sometimes a well-meaning single person will point out the final words of Matthew 19:12 and conclude, "Ray, I can't accept it." But wherever Scripture records this kind of statement, "He who is able to accept this, let him accept it," two things apply: (1) The word *he* is generic. Although one definition of *eunuch* is "a castrated male incapable of sexual intercourse," every unmarried Christian is called to be a "mental eunuch" for the sake of God's kingdom. In this case a eunuch is a single person committed to Christ and keeping his or her sexual appetite under control. (2) It makes sense only to Christians. This is emphasized in verse 11: "Not all men can accept this statement, but only those to whom it has been given."

Christians can stay moral because of the power of the Holy Spirit inside them. Have you unwrapped your gift?

Now you may want to trade in your gift for a husband or a wife, and the day may come when it's time to do so. But in the meantime recognize the tremendous advantages you have that you'll give up if you marry. Again, Paul wrote:

> My desire is to have you free from all anxiety and distressing care. The unmarried [man] is anxious about the things of the Lord, how he may please the Lord; but the married man is anxious about worldly matters, how he may please his wife. And he is drawn in diverging directions — his interests are divided, and he is distracted [from his devotion to God]. And the unmarried woman or girl is concerned and anxious about the matters of the Lord, how to be wholly separated and set apart in body and spirit; but the married woman has her cares [centered] in earthly affairs, how she may please her husband. Now I say this for your own welfare and profit, not to put (a halter of) restraint upon you, but to promote what is seemly and good order and to secure your undistracted and undivided devotion to the Lord (1 Cor. 7:32-35, Amplified).

Did you ever consider a man or woman worldly just because he or she wanted to please a wife or husband? The word *worldly* as used here doesn't necessarily mean sinful, but preoccupied with things that have no eternal value. Grocery shopping for one person is one thing; for two or more it's a different kind of trip. A married person's time is not his or her own. While one spouse might want to read, pray or work at the church, the other may ask for that block of time.

In 1 Corinthians 7:32-35 Paul is affirming the value of the single life. He's asking, "If you love Jesus, what are you doing right now that would be somewhat disrupted if you got married?" Someone reading this might say, "Well, I do love Jesus, but I'm not doing anything for Him, so marriage won't disrupt anything." Stop right there. If you love Him and aren't doing anything *for* Him, do you really think you'll serve the person you say you love? True love always begets service.

Don't misunderstand. Paul is not writing against marriage. But the grass *isn't* always greener on the other side of the fence, and marriage is sure to complicate your life. Paul is stressing the absolute urgency of making Jesus Christ your greatest love, whether you marry or not.

Single Blessings

Unless you are a single parent, your gift of singleness gives you very practical blessings you will lose the moment you marry.

1. *Mobility.* How many tickets does it take for a single person to go anywhere? One. From marriage on it takes two or more. As a single you can travel anywhere in the world at the cheapest price you'll ever pay. Oh, how I want to go on a photography safari in Africa. But if I ever do that, you can be sure I wouldn't go without my wife. That means it will cost me twice what it would cost a single person without children.

In his book *Singles Ask*, Harold Ivan Smith records a beautiful quote from physician and linguist Evelyn Ramsey, a missionary in Papua New Guinea:

> I realize now there would have been no way I could have read the books I've read, written the words I've written, gone to the places I've gone, studied the courses I have studied, learned the languages I have learned, maintained the schedule I have maintained, mended the people I have mended — if I had been encumbered by a husband and family.[4]

Ever wonder if God wants you to be a missionary? It's a terrible thing to feel God's call on your life and never fulfill it. Through one of several missionary organizations offering short-term missionary opportunities for people of any age, you can find out whether the missionary life is for you. One of the finest of these organizations is the interdenominational Youth With a Mission, which provides great biblical training and opportunities for ministry. One phone call could change your life forever. (Youth With a Mission, 75-5851 Kuakini Highway, Kailua-Kona, HI 96740; (808) 329-0588.)

Looking for something to do this summer? Maybe you know you're not meant to be a full-time missionary, but that doesn't mean you have to miss out on the possibility of doing some real missionary work. If you are over eighteen, you may be qualified to lead a Teen Missions team to nearly anywhere in the world. Maybe you've seen their advertising. Teen Missions builds orphanages, youth camps and so on, while singing in churches and witnessing on the world's streets. If you're ten to eighteen you can be a Teen Missions team member. To contact them write:

Teen Missions International, P.O. Box 1056, Merritt Island, FL 32952; (407) 453-0350.

2. *Self-development.* If you're going to be single for at least a season of your life, don't become a couch potato and let moss grow between your toes. Discover your potential. Develop your gifts fully. God has a great plan for your life. Ask Him to show you what that plan is. Then seek Him — spend quality and quantity time with Him to find His plan. As you do, you'll discover exactly where you fit in. Your talents will be a witness for the glory of Jesus Christ.

Even if you are a single parent, you have more free time than you would if you were married. If you are single and alone, praise God for your free time. If you ever marry, most of your free time will be gone. Right now you can learn anything you want to learn. Everything — from the care and feeding of aardvarks to the dangerous effects of zymurgy — is at your fingertips. (If you are going to raise aardvarks, please begin your occupation before you get married so your partner will understand the life ahead of him or her!)

I've mentioned your mobility. But bloom where you're planted. Things so often look better somewhere else until you get there.

For inspiration and a glimpse of the unending opportunities awaiting you, read Harold Ivan Smith's *A Singular Devotion: 366 Portraits of Singles Who Have Changed the World* (Fleming H. Revell). You too can make this world a better place. Go for it!

Caution Advised

In 1 Corinthians 7:26 (LB) Paul urges extreme caution about marrying at moments of peril:

> Here is the problem: We Christians are facing great dangers to our lives at present. In times like these I think it is best for a person to remain unmarried.

Paul himself was under great persecution for his faith in Christ. With prophetic eyes he looked ahead and saw the persecution the whole church would come under. Imagine the horror of having Roman soldiers drag your husband or wife out of your house. Imagine the torture of hearing that he or she was fed to a lion or burned as a human torch. That's the hideous pain Paul was urging unmarried Christians to avoid.

Of course, there are risks in any age, and the very nature of love causes the lover to be vulnerable to the pain of loss. But times of real crisis call for more caution.

As I write this book, America has recently concluded a war against Iraq. News reports abound about the disintegration that took place in marriages during this quick war. When one or both spouses are apart for many months, or even years, especially if they live under the constant danger of dying in battle, the stress often causes marriage casualties, too. That's the kind of thing Paul is warning against. Military marriages are difficult — but not impossible. Anyone in the military or marrying someone in the military needs to be realistic about the strain such a marriage will undoubtedly put on their lives. Such marriages, in order to last, generally require two very mature Christians who are completely sold out to the Lord and each other.

However, even in Paul's dreadful times he made no dogmatic or absolute statement about Christian singles staying single. After advising unmarried people to stay single, he wrote, "And this I say for your own benefit; not to put a restraint upon you, but to promote what is seemly, and to secure undistracted devotion to the Lord" (1 Cor. 7:35).

And in 1 Corinthians 7:9 (LB) he says, "But if you can't control yourselves, go ahead and marry. It is better to marry than to burn with lust." Unrepented sexual immorality is a sin that leads to hell (Heb. 13:4; Rev. 21:8; 22:14-15). But the word *burn* in the above verse is the Greek word *puroo*, and it means "to burn out unfulfilled." Paul clearly understood the power of the human sex drive, and he knew that one of God's reasons for humans to marry is to fulfill that drive within the bounds of morality (1 Cor. 7:2).

You're Not as Unusual as You May Think

Whatever your age, don't give in to the self-pity that you're alone — the only forgotten one. In 1990 nearly two in five American adults were single. That means sixty-six million single Americans. To bring that number in focus, that's approximately the *combined* population of New York, Pennsylvania, Ohio, Michigan, New Jersey, Massachusetts and Connecticut. While the percent of married-couple households continues to decline, the number of single and single-parent households continues to grow. Single adults now make up 50 percent of big-city populations.

According to researcher George Barna, "At some point early in the next century, the majority of America will be single."[5]

The study of nationwide marriage and divorce statistics reveals a fact not often understood: First marriages that have the best chance of lasting a lifetime are "older" marriages. For a woman, statistics turn around at age twenty-eight; the longer she waits after that, the better her chance for a lifetime marriage. For a man, the magic age is thirty. Why? Because by the time women are twenty-eight

37

and men are thirty, they generally know what they want for the rest of their lives and what kind of people they want to live with for the rest of their lives.

Upon hearing this news, a woman might object: But all the eligible men will be married by that time! Yes, in the United States there are some ten million more women than men over age twenty-five. But there are 4,814,000 never-married men between the ages of twenty-five and thirty-four and only 2,942,000 women.

Horror stories abound concerning the slim chance a mature woman has of marrying. But these grim stories are usually based on a flawed study done by Yale and Harvard universities. Even the Yale-Harvard researchers now admit their projections were far too extreme. The truth is, since 1978 first-marriage rates for women in their late thirties have increased by 37 percent. Of all American men over the age of eighteen, 25 percent have never married.

Barbara Lovenheim's book *Beating the Marriage Odds: When You Are Smart, Single and Over 35* (Morrow) exposes the mistakes made by the Yale-Harvard study and makes new projections, gleaned from the National Center of Health Statistics, based on 1987 marriage rates: At age forty, a woman who has never been married has nearly a one in four chance of being married. A never-married man at forty has nearly a one in three chance of being married. The Census Bureau estimates that nine out of ten Americans will eventually marry.

Why should a woman consider waiting for marriage until she's twenty-eight — or a man until he's thirty? Most people change immensely between the ages of eighteen and twenty-eight. At least in their thought patterns, the change is often as dramatic as was the change between ages eight and eighteen. Jesus waited until He was thirty to begin His public ministry, because the Jewish people considered no one in his twenties truly mature.

Timothy Wasn't a Kid

As parents, Arlyne and I have raised three of our own children and several others from broken homes. On each child's sixteenth birthday we shared the tradition of having him or her recite and then thoroughly discuss 1 Timothy 4:12: "Let no one look down on your youthfulness, but rather in speech, conduct, love, faith and purity, show yourself an example of those who believe."

Many Christians are surprised that the word *youthfulness* in this verse would be better translated "singleness." Timothy was no kid. He wasn't a teen or even a man in his twenties when Paul addressed two epistles to him. No man under the age of thirty would then have been thought mature enough to be an apostolic representative and, therefore, head of all the presbyters in the churches of Ephesus and nearby communities.

Any person who lives by the guidance set forth in 1 Timothy 4:12 will be able to maintain a Christian testimony and stay morally pure in these immoral times. Here's why:

- "speech" = what you say
- "conduct" = what you do
- "love" = choosing to do God's highest good
- "faith" = trusting God and living by His Word
- "purity" = staying moral in thought, word and action

A Christian at any age is God's representative and witness here on earth. The ingredients of godly speech, conduct, love, faith and purity are absolutely essential to maintain that witness. "Let no one look down on your singleness." No one, not even you.

Seeking What and Whom?

In 1 Corinthians 7 Paul gives another clear word to singles — and married people: "Are you bound to a wife? Do not seek to be free. Are you free from a wife? Do not seek a wife" (1 Cor. 7:27, Amplified).

That's the watchword: do not seek. Do not seek means don't run after marriage, chasing it as a dog would chase a rabbit! Though you may have every desire to marry someone (and that's a normal, healthy feeling), don't rush out to find marriage at all costs. Relax! It's wise to remember that God brought Eve to Adam. Adam didn't go hunting for a wife. In fact, he was asleep at the moment God was bringing Eve to him.

In *God's Call to the Single Adult*, Mike Cavanaugh writes:

> God is calling you to be content in Him first. He is calling you to look to Him in your loneliness, in your sexual struggles, and in your feelings of rejection and hurt. He is calling you to be complete in Him.
>
> "But, Mike, doesn't Proverbs say somewhere that 'he who finds a wife, finds a good thing'?"
>
> "Yes. That's Proverbs 18:22."
>
> "Well, how am I supposed to find a wife (or husband) if I don't look for one?"
>
> Good point. At least on the surface. This verse does seem to indicate the value of searching for a mate, doesn't it? There's just one problem, though. The word "find" in the Hebrew doesn't mean "to find by searching for." It means "to *discover* along the way." This verse is saying, "If you're wrapped up with the Lord, submitting to Him and

serving Him according to His will, and along comes someone who ends up being your mate, that's a good thing."[6]

Did you ever play hide and seek? Everyone else hides while the person who is "it" counts to ten. "Ready or not, here I come!" Then "it" dashes off in any direction, hunting down anyone to tag and make "it." That's no way to approach marriage. You don't want just any "it" for a lifetime partner — not if you have any desire for lasting happiness.

Referring to 1 Corinthians 7:27, the late Alan Redpath wrote that the command not to seek "stands in refreshing contrast to the frenzied search for a life partner which is conducted by many people today. When one witnesses the frantic efforts by some to find a mate, one can only trust that the person who is the victim of such an assault has regained enough emotional stability to be able to conduct a strategic withdrawal immediately, before he or she becomes deeply involved in the situation. Much wreckage has been caused by the tactics of a person who seeks a life partner at *any* price."[7]

Here's a good test. Can you say what Paul said: "Not that I speak in regard to need, for I have learned in whatever state I am, to be content" (Phil. 4:11, NKJV)?

Paul said he could be content single or married, with or without money, in prison for his faith or out. Can you? Aside from all earthly matters or people, how deeply committed are you to Jesus Christ? Is He Lord, absolute boss, of your life? Does He call the shots — or do you call your own?

If Jesus Christ really is Lord of your life, you will be content right now to be wherever He has put you, remembering "God causes all things to work together for good to those who love God, to those who are called according to His purpose" (Rom. 8:28). Even prison "worked good" for Paul. If you feel you are in the prison of circumstances beyond your control *because you are being obedient to Jesus Christ as directed by His Word*, then what's happening *will work good*. Trust the Lord, keep on obeying Him, and your future is guaranteed to work good (Prov. 3:5-8; Rom. 10:11).

Fischer and O'Neill add keen insight here:

> What God wants us to pursue is not marriage, but love. If we're pursuing marriage in our dating, we're pursuing the wrong thing. We start making up our own ideas of what love is. We don't allow the Lord to show us and teach us what love actually is through the relationships He gives us. "Pursue love," the Bible says, "not marriage." This is a simple principle, but it set me free in the past few months in my relationships with Christian sisters.[8]

There is one bottom-line reason to get married. If other factors don't rest on this base, stop. Ready to read it? Here goes: If the two of you can serve God better married to each other than the two of you could serve God singly, then, with all other reasons in total alignment with God's Word and both your hearts, you have a great reason to get married.

God's Will?

Again, if you are single, reach out and embrace God's gift to you. Hold before you the model of Jesus Christ, who never married. At the same time, remain open to God's direction. Don't declare you're *absolutely never* going to marry. I recently met one ninety-five-year-old woman who introduced me to her ninety-two-year-old husband. Newlyweds! She told me, "I've been a widow for more than thirty years. I just *knew* I'd never get married again. I told everybody I wouldn't." Then she pinched his cheek and said, "But he's so cute!"

You don't know what God has in store for you — at any age. But, as Romans 8:28 says,

If you love God,
you can count on it that it's going
to turn out for good.

Questions for Reflection and Discussion

1. Write an answer to the letter preceding this chapter. Should "Over the Hill at Thirty-two" remain "in a panic"?

2. Read 1 Corinthians 7:7 in the Living Bible. Now look up the word "gift" in the dictionary. Have you ever thought of singleness as a gift? If someone who loves you unconditionally gave you a gift, wouldn't you try to use that gift to its greatest potential? Who gives you the gift of being able to stay "happily unmarried" according to this verse?

3. Meditate on 1 Corinthians 7:27 (Amplified). What does the admonition "do not seek a wife (or husband)" mean to you? Contrast this verse with Genesis 2:18 where God said, "It is not good for the man to be alone."

4. In a practical sense, what does it mean to pursue love, not marriage, in relationships with others? How would it be done? Write your answer on paper and discuss it.

5. Take another close look at the three main areas of blessings you will lose if you trade in your singleness for a lifetime partner. Discuss how marriage would affect each of these areas. Why would it be worth it? Why would it not be worth it?

Dear Ray,

I've made so many mistakes — it may be a mistake to write you. I will be at your Singles Plus seminar next month. I plan to talk with you then so you won't have to write back now. I am eager to hear you because I want to know if you have any answers for me. To give you a quick history: My folks fought all the time I was growing up and finally divorced when I was fifteen. It really tore me apart — both the fighting and the divorce (but the divorce hurt the most). My dad doesn't come around much.

My mom is a Christian; my dad never has been. I am, but I'm having a tough time staying close to God. I've dated a bunch of guys (very few Christians, and those that said they were *weren't*). They all wanted my body, not me. (I've failed God twice in that regard.) Ray, I'm beginning to hate men. Even though I'll be at your seminar, I don't know whether I want to date ever again. I'm sure I don't want to get married. Are there some things you could tell me about how to get close to God when you've made the kind of mistakes I've made? I don't feel called to be a nun. But I hurt so bad, and I need Jesus to do something quick.

Used and Abused

*But O my soul, don't be
discouraged. Don't be upset.
Expect God to act!
For I know that I shall again
have plenty of reason to praise him
for all that he will do.
He is my help! He is my God!*
                              Psalm 42:11, LB

TWO

BECOMING WHOLE

Christians grow taller by kneeling.

I n *Straightforward: Why Wait Till Marriage?* Larry Tomczak writes on the wholeness God desires for His people: " 'Saved' means to be made whole, and if you are not an integral part of a body you cannot ever be completely whole (or saved) (Matt. 1:21; 1 Cor. 1:18, RSV). One only becomes whole in fellowship where we can learn to live as functioning members of the kingdom counter-culture."[1]

God wants you to be a whole — unbroken — person. And wholeness includes healthy relationships with members of both sexes.

A Model of Wholeness

Paul says we are to be like Jesus: "For from the very beginning God decided that those who came to him — and all along he knew who would — should become like his Son, so that his Son would be the First, with many brothers" (Rom. 8:29, LB).

Though Jesus never dated, was never engaged and never married, He was the most mentally healthy person who has ever lived. He cared deeply about women and did not isolate Himself from the opposite sex. Let's look at His relationships with women.

John 4 gives us a picture of Him talking to an outcast Samaritan woman, and because He did, a whole city came to understand who He was. Another day He stopped the hemorrhage of a woman who'd been unclean and untouchable for twelve years (Luke 8:43-48).

For a grieving widow He brought a son back from the dead (Luke 7:12-15). For a wife and husband He brought a daughter from death to life (Luke 8:49-56). No woman was more thankful to our Lord than an adulteress about to be stoned. Jesus stepped in, saved her life and told her, "Go your way. From now on sin no more" (John 8:11).

Jesus and His disciples traveled and ministered with godly women who often helped to support their ministry financially (Luke 8:1-3).

Was He ever tempted sexually? Certainly. Hebrews 4:15 says He was "one who has been tempted in all things as we are." The verse continues, "...yet without sin." Christ knew how to take "every thought captive" (2 Cor. 10:5).

There were more women in Jesus' sphere of relationships: sisters Mary and Martha, two of his closest friends (John 11:1-45). Though these two didn't always understand our Lord (John 11:20-33), they always loved Him.

You May Not Feel Whole

God created every human to love and to need love. Your first efforts at getting love were most likely directed toward your mom and dad. You were either a hit or a miss. Even if you were a hit when you first arrived, a younger brother or sister may have stolen your parents' affections. One parent — or both — may have been working so hard they lost track of loving you. Dad or Mom may have been drinking excessively or too involved in their own activities.

In America at least one in five men and one in three women have been victims of childhood or teenage sexual abuse (one of the least reported crimes in America). Is it any wonder we find so many women-haters or men-haters in our society? These people don't need dates, lovers or marriage. They need help.

46

If uncivil war was a regular event in your childhood home, you may have taken the blame yourself. Other people who've lived through a difficult past blame every bad thing they do on their parents. After all, they didn't ask to be born into this "crummy" world. They feel the world should make it up to them. Sometimes their hostility is loud and overt; sometimes it is stuffed down inside and hardly identifiable.

These hurting people either don't know how to or *won't* let God deal with their problems; they mask their emotions, set their own rules and become their own gods. When they find it impossible to even the score with anyone who does them wrong, they find substitutes with whom they can get even, though the substitutes have no causal relationship to the original problem. Hence, bitter men use and abuse women, and bitter women use and abuse men. They may strike with words or fists. Or, because of their bitterness, these persons gratify their lust with another's body. But sex never fills the emptiness inside them. They don't feel loved. (Bitterness and love can never reside in the same person at the same time.)

Without God, many people attempt to become their own "god," making their own rules about life. The book of Jude fully describes these "god-persons." The attitude of a god-person is this: I need to be loved. I'll get someone to love me. I'll get someone's kisses, touch, body. I'll prove I'm lovable enough to have that person give him or herself to me. The sad thing is, the one being used doesn't feel as if he or she is being used. In fact, there are certain men and far more women who are suckers for the god-person. They feel it's their personal responsibility to love the god-person and make up for whatever they missed in childhood.

Please realize that no matter how hard you try, you can't take God's place in anybody's life. If you attempt to do that, you will only end up terribly frustrated and in great emotional pain. The emptiness any human feels can only be met by the Holy Spirit when they honestly surrender their life to Jesus Christ.

No matter what your circumstances, if you are your own god-person, Jesus Christ exists to fill the emptiness in you (Luke 4:16-18). No matter how numerous your problems or how deep your emotional pain, you will never be alone if Jesus Christ is with you.

Fear, Not Faith

It is *fear* and not *faith* that keeps some people from ever dating or having healthy relationships. To these Paul would say what he said to Timothy: "For God has not given us a spirit of timidity, but of power and love and discipline" (2 Tim. 1:7). Timidity destroys the joy of being with other people. The self-conscious person is too worried about how he or she is coming across to be good company. Timidity does not come from God. But these characteristics do: (1) power (the inner knowledge that Christ is in you; whenever you enter a room, loving royalty enters that room); (2) love (*agapao*, God's kind of love that always chooses to do God's highest good for everyone); (3) discipline (the denying of selfish feelings or lusts and obedience to God's Word).

Power. Love. Discipline. They're the marks of a mature, whole Christian. What steps can you take to become whole?

Who Am I?

There's a basic question every Christian needs to ask several times a day: Who am I now that Christ is Lord of my life? The magnificent answer is that God has "delivered us from the domain of darkness, and transferred us to the kingdom of His beloved Son" (Col. 1:13). You are royalty!

"Beloved, now we are children of God, and it has not appeared as yet what we shall be" (1 John 3:2). You may have had an earthly father who greatly disappointed you. But you have another Father: " 'And do not call anyone on earth your father; for One is your Father, He who is in heaven' " (Matt. 23:9). If you're a Christian, you're God's kid. Don't let your feelings become stronger than God's Word in your life.

Sometimes our old habit patterns get in the way of doing what God wants. Even Paul fought this frustration. He wrote, "For that which I am doing, I do not understand; for I am not practicing what I would like to do, but I am doing the very thing I hate" (Rom. 7:15).

Because Jesus Christ died for you (John 3:16), conquered death (Heb. 2:14-15) and rose from the grave (Luke 24:1-9), you can shout what Paul shouted: "Thanks be to God through Jesus Christ our Lord!" (Rom. 7:25). Christ is your deliverer from both your sin and the curse of your sin (1 John 1:9-2:6).

If you are God's kid, "pursue righteousness, godliness, faith, love, perseverance and gentleness. Fight the good fight of faith; take hold of the eternal life to which you were called, and you made the good confession in the presence of many witnesses" (1 Tim. 6:11-12). Keep on keeping on with Christ. If you do, "When He appears, we shall be like Him, because we shall see Him just as He is" (1 John 3:2).

The "Who Am I?" question is answered as one studies God's Word, prays and fellowships with His people. Calvin Miller notes:

> Jesus instructed us to pray by separating ourselves from others and entering the closet. Could it be Christ wanted us to discover something about who we are and what we might become if we could free ourselves from the necessity of always being with other people?

Shutting the closet door behind us is not only necessary for prayer; it is necessary for the finding of character....

Our real problem is liking ourselves enough to want to be alone.[2]

Of course, not all discoveries about ourselves will take place when we are alone. Rich Buhler, whose Christian counsel is given to callers daily on his nationally broadcast radio program "Table Talk," adds this:

In order to develop a more realistic self-image we must be willing to talk to those who know us best or with others who are in the position to give us accurate feedback.... Our hunger for *worth* is the reason we are concerned with our self-image. What value is there to the fact that I exist? To whom am I valuable? What can I do to improve my value?[3]

Stop a moment and contemplate this staggering truth: If you had been the only human being on this planet, Jesus Christ would still have come here and died for you. *You* are uniquely valuable to Him. He seeks an intimate relationship with *you.* No other relationship will ever come near to equaling the relationship possible with God. Yet God doesn't want you to close yourself off from others.

Forgive Yourself

You can't unscramble scrambled eggs! Neither can you go back one half-minute in your life and undo the past. But you can recover. You can be completely forgiven or healed. But your memory will be less kind to you than God will be. The devil, "the accuser of our brethren" (Rev. 12:10), will make sure you're reminded of every failure. That's why, as far as possible, you must never do anything that will give you deep regret. Even then God will hear your heart if you honestly seek His power to quit that sin forever and if you are deeply sorry for what your sin has done to your relationship with Him (Ps. 51:1-17; Jer. 29:13; 1 John 1:9-2:6).

Many regretted sins may have happened before you knew Jesus Christ as Lord. But if Jesus Christ is your Lord, you have been born again (John 3:3,5). "Therefore if any man [person] is in Christ, he is a new creature; the old things passed away; behold, new things have come" (2 Cor. 5:17)

One day someone came to Martin Luther's door and asked, "Does Martin Luther live here?" Luther answered, "No. Martin Luther is dead. Christ lives here now!" (Rom. 6:4.) Just like the old gray mare, you ain't what you used to be!

If you are trying to please Christ, you are not condemned (Rom. 8:1). Furthermore, "a righteous man falls seven times, and rises again" (Prov. 24:16). All of us fall at times. New Christians especially tend to stumble because the devil is so angry they've left him. He tries to trip them up. But think of it this way: When a baby stumbles and falls, you write it down in a baby book because you're pleased the little one was trying to walk. When a Christian falls, God doesn't say, "Well, I'll scratch that one off my list!" A fallen child calls out for help to its father; our Father God stands ready to help all of His children stand up. The Holy Spirit grieves when someone falls spiritually and then wallows in sin or self-pity, refusing to let Him set them free.

Melody Green writes in her tract *But I Can't Forgive Myself*:

> If someone else with a situation like yours came to you for counsel, what advice would you give them? Is it easier for you to grab onto God's forgiveness for someone else than it is to believe for yourself? Perhaps you are harder on yourself than on others. Remember that God is no respecter of persons. To believe one thing for someone else and another thing for yourself is inconsistent. Beliefs like that are based on *feelings* not on *truth*. Sometimes when I "blow it" I feel so hurt and disappointed in myself that it's hard to receive forgiveness, yet I would firmly tell someone else in my position to stand on the truth of the Bible.... If God has forgiven us, we set ourselves above Him when we reject His gift.[4]

It doesn't matter what you used to be. It doesn't matter what you are the day you give your life to Christ. It matters totally what you will become.

Forgive Those Who Have Harmed You

In Romans 8:29 Paul tells us we are to be like Jesus. This applies to all areas of our spiritual life, but here let's deal with one specific area: His willingness to forgive those who had let Him down or done Him wrong.

As He was dying our Lord looked at those responsible and said, "Father, forgive them; for they do not know what they are doing" (Luke 23:34).

Your father may have abandoned you as a kid. A stepfather may have beaten or raped you. But Jesus says, "For if you forgive men [mankind] for their transgressions, your heavenly Father will also forgive you. But if you do not forgive men, then your Father will not forgive your transgressions" (Matt. 6:14-15).

Suppose you can't reconcile with your parents. Suppose one or both are dead or purposely avoiding you. Suppose either or both are so violent or drugged or drunk or sold out to sin that it would be dangerous to be with them. Then pray for them and forgive them. Write to them if possible, expressing Christ's love.

A look at Jesus' friends shows the frail nature of humanity and the need for continual forgiveness:

> Then Jesus came with them to a place called Gethsemane, and said to His disciples, "Sit here while I go over there and pray." And He took with Him Peter and the two sons of Zebedee, and began to be grieved and distressed. Then He said to them, "My soul is deeply grieved, to the point of death; remain here and keep watch with Me" (Matt. 26:36-38).

What request could have been more reasonable to ask of your closest friends? Jesus knew He was about to be crucified. But that didn't distress Him as much as the coming moment when His Father would turn His back on Him because of your sins and mine.

> And He went a little beyond them, and fell on His face and prayed, saying, "My Father, if it is possible, let this cup pass from Me; yet not as I will, but as Thou wilt." And He came to the disciples and found them sleeping, and said to Peter, "So, you men could not keep watch with Me for one hour? Keep watching and praying, that you may not enter into temptation; the spirit is willing, but the flesh is weak" (Matt. 26:39-41).

At this moment when Jesus most needed His friends to stand with Him, they fell asleep. They failed to sense His grief. They yawned at His despair, a snore in God's pained face.

What *could* Christ have done if He had lost His temper? He who withered a fig tree with His words (Mark 11:21) could have withered His friends. He who could cast a mountain into the sea with one sentence (Mark 11:23) could have cast these characters into the sea. But no such blast came from His mouth, just a loving word of disappointment and a warning.

Think of how Christ could have prayed. "Destroy Peter, James and John, Father. They've failed Me. They're hypocrites. Keep them from My sight forever. Torture them in hell." Instead, He prayed a word we see Him pray no other place but Gethsemane: *if*.

"He went away again a second time and prayed, saying, 'My Father, if this cannot pass away unless I drink it, Thy will be done' " (Matt. 26:42).

The story continues:

> And again He came and found them sleeping, for their eyes were heavy.

And He left them again, and went away and prayed a third time, saying the same thing once more. Then He came to the disciples, and said to them, "Are you still sleeping and taking your rest? Behold, the hour is at hand and the Son of Man is being betrayed into the hands of sinners. Arise, let us be going; behold, the one who betrays Me is at hand" (Matt. 26:43-46).

Failure. Utter failure. No one knows what would have happened had these disciples stayed awake and prayed through the night. Peter might never have denied Christ. None of them might have experienced the great fear that seized them after Jesus' death (John 20:19). They might even have understood what was happening while it was happening!

Any human will fail you at times. You'll need them, and they won't be there for you. That's not how it should be. It's how it is. But God says He won't forgive you if you won't forgive others (Matt. 6:14-15). So forgiveness isn't really something you do for others. It's a vital thing you do for yourself. Never wish pain or disaster on anyone, no matter how much that person has hurt you. Hate hurts the hater far more than it hurts the hated (Matt. 18:34-35). Forgive — and live.

Abraham Lincoln was known to hold short accounts. Someone once asked him, "Why do you try to make friends out of your enemies?" Lincoln replied, "Am I not destroying my enemies when I make them my friends?"

To be a forgiven, whole person, you need to "let all bitterness and wrath and anger and clamor and slander be put away from you, along with all malice. And be kind to one another, tender-hearted, forgiving each other, just as God in Christ also has forgiven you" (Eph. 4:31-32).

If it seems impossible to forgive someone for wrongs done to you, don't hesitate to seek professional help from a godly counselor or pastor. Also available are my cassette "How to Forgive" and Arlyne's tape "How to Get Rid of Your Anger." You can order them through our Marriage Plus office.

Act Upon God's Word — Not Your Feelings

God demands that we act upon His Word (Matt. 7:24-27; Heb. 5:13-14; James 1:22).

Many of the things God tells us to do in His Word don't feel natural. For example, "Consider it all joy, my brethren, when you encounter various trials" (James 1:2). Now come on. If you're facing problems, do you want to rejoice? Aren't your feelings telling you to mope or cry or have a pity-party? Yet God means what He says. Consider the story of Paul and Silas. Bloody and beaten, there they were lying in a prison at midnight, not swearing or snoring, but "singing hymns of praise to God" (Acts 16:22-26)!

During the first weeks and months after I discovered the Bible had answers for my "horrible" marriage, I often felt like running away rather than showing inner strength when something went wrong. No Scripture passage helped me more than Matthew 7:24-27, especially the phrase "act upon the word."

I knew God promised that if I acted upon His Word, our home would withstand the storms of life. He promises the same thing for every single Christian's home. *Acting* means "to perform a role." The role God calls us to perform is a positive, confident role because He is our strength (Ps. 46:1). We have to *act* because, until we grasp that He really is sustaining us while working out His promise to us, we will at times feel insecure. Even the most mature Christians have moments of insecurity — until we remember God's promises and put our trust back in His hands.

Paul was transformed from a militant enemy of the church to its major spiritual leader, and many people assume he grew mature and full of power overnight. But after his conversion Paul spent fourteen years on the backside of a desert, growing in the Lord (Gal. 1:15-2:2). Then he became a church leader. We know very little about that time except that he received direct revelation from Jesus Christ and came away fully versed and in total agreement with the Old Testament, yet in total spiritual alignment with the New Testament Scripture writers.

Was Paul happy while he waited in the desert? A great deal of his spiritual growth was no doubt painful. He had to maintain his Jewish faith yet die to his religious tradition. He had found the Messiah but lost his earthly friends. He was living with the camels, having fallen from high honors among his peers. How did he deal with "forgetting what lies behind and reaching forward to what lies ahead" (Phil. 3:13)? Paul simply pressed "on toward the goal for the prize of the upward call of God in Christ Jesus" (Phil. 3:14).

Happiness is a by-product of obedience to Jesus Christ. In the short term, directions from God may not seem to make one happy. But in the long term, happiness will come if God's directions are followed (John 8:31-32).

When Joshua replaced Moses as the leader who would take God's people into the promised land, God told Joshua to study His Word "day and night" and to "be careful to do according to all that is written in it; for then you will make your way prosperous, and then you will have success" (Josh. 1:8). What He's done for others, He'll do for you. Act upon God's Word.

Keep Releasing God's Love

When our daughter, Bethany, was about six, she brought four beautiful autumn leaves into the house. She handed one to Arlyne and said, "I love you, Mommy."

She handed one to me and said, "I love you, Daddy." She handed out the two remaining leaves, one to each of her brothers, and said, "I love you, Tim and David." She looked at her empty hands for a moment and into our smiling faces. Then she looked into a mirror and said, "That felt good. I love you, Bethany!" Real love does feel good.

Christians grow into maturity by learning to give and not just receive. Many people spend their whole lives running away from life. Want to feel good about life? Help someone. Volunteer to work with your church, a nearby ministry, Campus Crusade for Christ, Chi Alpha, Youth for Christ, Young Life, the Red Cross, the local hospital. Don't sit moping or feeling sorry for yourself. Reach out and fill someone's life with Christ's love. "Give, and it will be given to you; good measure, pressed down, shaken together, running over, they will pour into your lap. For by your standard of measure it will be measured to you in return" (Luke 6:38).

Larry Tomczak writes:

> Serving is the foundation of our Lord's life and the life of His body. God is after a serving spirit. We will never outgrow serving. In fact, it is the gift of the Spirit as seen in [Romans 12:7]. Imagine, the ability to fix cars, help people budget, babysit in a time of need, and simply do little things for others is a supernatural gift from God! Then one day upon entering marriage we take that servant spirit with us — which is the basis for a happy home in Christ.[5]

Have you ever asked yourself why Jesus Christ chose to save you? The answer is in Ephesians 2:8-10:

> For by grace you have been saved through faith; and that not of yourselves, it is the gift of God; not as a result of works, that no one should boast. For we are His workmanship, created in Christ Jesus for good works, which God prepared beforehand, that we should walk in them.

Jesus saved you to do His "good works." Fail to do Christ's good works, and you will miss the entire purpose for your life. As you walk toward wholeness, you'll reach out to others, showing them God's love through your good works.

God's Word to All Singles

As I've ministered over the years, I have been given copies of the following message for singles. Some of the copies have said this was a loving word to a son from an anonymous father expressing God's will. Other copies said it is a prophetic word spoken to a large group of singles. I do not know who voiced it here on earth, but it is profound, and I'm sure it agrees with the heart of God:

Everyone longs to give himself completely to someone, to have a deep soul relationship with another — to be loved thoroughly and exclusively.

But God says to a Christian: "Not until you are satisfied, fulfilled and content with being loved by Me alone — with giving yourself totally and unreservedly to Me; with having an intensely personal and unique relationship with Me alone, discovering that only in Me is your satisfaction to be found — will you be capable of the perfect human relationship that I have planned for you. You will never be united with another until you are united with Me — exclusive of anyone or anything else, exclusive of any other desires or longings.

I want you to stop planning, stop wishing, and allow Me to give you the most thrilling plan existing — one that you cannot imagine. I want you to have the best. Please allow Me to bring it to you. You just keep watching Me, expecting the greatest things. Keep experiencing the satisfaction that I am. Keep listening and learning the things that I tell you. You just wait, that's all. Don't be anxious. Don't worry.

Don't look around at the things others have gotten or that I've given them. Don't look around at the things you think you want. You just keep looking at Me, or you will miss what I want to show you. And then, when you are ready, I'll surprise you with a love far more wonderful than any you would dream of. You see, until you are ready, and until the one I have for you is ready — (I am working even at this moment to have both of you ready at the same time) — until you are both satisfied exclusively with Me, and the life prepared for you, you won't be able to experience the love that exemplifies your relationship with Me, and this is the perfect love. And, dear one, I want you to have this most wonderful love. I want you to see in the flesh a picture of your relationship with Me, and to enjoy materially and concretely the everlasting union of beauty, perfection and love. What I offer you is Myself. Know that I love you utterly. I am God. Believe it and be satisfied.

Note: As this chapter ends, I would like to recommend a book that will help you walk through healing of the past. The book is *Lifetime Guarantee: Making*

Your Christian Life Work, and What to Do When It Doesn't by Bill Gillham (Wolgemuth & Hyatt). Anyone in need of inner healing will find this book extremely helpful.

Good resolutions and babies crying
during church service have one thing in common.
They both need to be carried out at once!

Questions for Reflection and Discussion

1. Meditate on 2 Timothy 1:7. Why is this verse so important to understand in relation to developing friendships or as you approach other tasks? Is there a difference between natural inhibitions and "a spirit of fear"? Read Haggai 2:5. On what truth do we need to focus in order to lose any fear? Is there a healthy fear? Read 2 Corinthians 7:1 for the answer.

2. The Lord longs to give us an abundant life, while Satan wants just the opposite (John 10:10). In order to have that abundant life we must be "conformed to the image of Christ" (Rom. 8:29) by exposing ourselves to the truth of God's Son and obeying His Word. Does having an abundant life mean you will always *feel* happy? What is the difference between "happiness" and "joy"? Contrast Jonah 4:6 with Jonah 4:8, then contrast Hebrews 12:2 with James 1:2-4 for your answers.

3. The goal of every Christian (single or married) who loves the Lord is to obey Him (John 14:15). As we obey Christ by seeking Him first and then doing His will, "all these things [including joy and other practical needs] will be added unto you" (Matt. 6:33). Carefully read Philippians 3:13-14. What do these verses say to you about not dwelling on the hurts of the past, rather seeking (pressing toward spiritual maturity) the "prize to which God in Jesus Christ is calling us upward"? Does God say that the "prize" will come without "trials"? What is the purpose of trials in our lives according to James 1:3? How valuable is "endurance"?

4. Have you been around people who seem to have inferiority complexes even when there is no apparent reason for it? If these people are Christians, how do you think their relationship with God is affected by feelings of inferiority? What do you feel is the root cause of feelings of inferiority? How can you guard against these feelings in yourself?

5. Some people feel they will only be mature *after* they get married. Others feel they will never be mature enough to *get* married. What is the difference between striving for maturity and striving for perfection? How can you really know if you *are* mature enough to get married? According to this chapter, what are some steps to take that will lead to maturity? Write down your answers and discuss them.

Dear Ray,

I'm a student at a Christian college. The women in my dorm, all between the ages of eighteen and twenty-six, want to know a bunch of things from you:

1. How do you know you're going to enjoy the guy you're dating? Are there things we could do to make dating fun and not a wrestling match, trying to preserve our virginity?

2. How important is dating anyway? Is it biblical? If so, could you give some biblical guidelines?

3. One girl in our dorm is dating a really nice guy, but he's unsaved. The truth is, most of us think he's nicer than the guys going to our school. What's wrong with that, if anything?

4. I almost didn't put this in, but a number of the girls want me to ask you: Two of them wear diaphragms. They can't get pregnant. Another of them is on the pill. Why would sex outside marriage be wrong if they can't get pregnant?

Women Wanting to Have Fun

*If you want favor
with both God and man,
and a reputation for good
judgment and common sense,
then trust the Lord completely;
don't ever trust yourself.
In everything you do, put God first,
and he will direct you and
crown your efforts with success.*
                    Proverbs 3:4-6, LB

THREE

THE DATING GAME

Some singles never want dates.
They want raisins.

W hen I was a kid, I learned to ride a bicycle the hard way. My parents couldn't afford a bike my size, but they got a great bargain on an adult-sized bike. So I tried. My feet barely touched the pedals, and I couldn't stop it by just stepping off. To get up on the bike, I had to be lifted onto the seat. Nevertheless, I was thrilled to have the bicycle.

My mom taught me how to ride it: She'd stay outside our house, and I'd ride around the block. Then she'd stand in front of the slowing bicycle and stop it so I could get off. In a day or so I got quite comfortable on the bike and had total confidence in Mom, the stopper. As my confidence in bike riding increased, I'd stay on the bike for longer rides. Mom would stay in the house. When I was finally too pooped to continue, I'd head for home and yell at the top of my lungs, "M-O-M-M-M-M-M-Y." She'd come running out to stop me.

All went great for a couple of days, until she got a phone call. I rode on and on in happiness, unaware my stopper had been stopped. Finally I was exhausted. I headed for home and the security of "M-O-M-M-M-M-M-Y." I yelled, but no Mom appeared. I circled the block again and hollered. No Mom. Twelve circles later, I faced the facts: Mom had gone deaf. I stopped pedaling, stuck out my right leg, leaned the bike over and fell off. From that time on until I grew tall enough to master it, that's how I always stopped. Bruised body or not, I love bicycle riding to this day. But let me tell you, there are easier ways to learn to ride a bicycle.

There are many ways to learn something worth learning. Some of the ways are very painful. You can learn through pain. But there is usually a far better way. It's my prayer that what I share in this chapter about dating will keep you from a great deal of unnecessary pain.

What Is a Date?

The clearest definition I've yet seen of the word *date* is "an appointment between two persons of the opposite sex for the mutual enjoyment of some form of social activity."

Casually dating just anyone who asks for a date or who catches your eye can be a serious mistake you'll have to live with for a lifetime. Jeremiah 17:9 warns:

The heart is more deceitful than all else
and is desperately sick;
Who can understand it?

Millions of couples have married even though at least one of them knew the match was wrong. Jeremiah 17:10 follows:

I, the Lord, search the heart,
I test the mind,
Even to give to each man according to his ways,
According to the results of his deeds.

As I mentioned before, the love of God is unconditional, but the blessings of God are totally conditional. If you want to live in God's blessings, you have to say no to the flow and be cool with the rule. If Jesus Christ is really your king, you'll submit to His kingship in your life (Matt. 7:21-23).

A date has significance. It means something. I'm married. Suppose you knew that but saw me dating some other woman. Would that *mean* something to you? It should!

Many single people complain to me that they dated someone just one time and were immediately asked by church or school friends, "Are you two going steady?" They ask that question because a date means something.

For a male, dating means several things. For one, it's a way to learn the financial responsibilities he'll carry if he becomes a Christian husband. First Timothy 5:8 tells us, "But if anyone does not provide for *his* own, and especially for those of *his* household, *he* has denied the faith, and is worse than an unbeliever" (italics mine). The male or female who ignores this command from God through Paul is immediately weakening the possibilities of having a biblical marriage. With rare exception guys should pay for their dates. To the man's birthday outing or in a rare moment when she knows he doesn't have the cash, a female might treat a man she's dated frequently. But this should not become a habit.

Going Dutch treat on dates usually gets the female in Dutch! She can be considered too eager or too independent to be taken seriously as a potential marriage partner.

After hearing me teach this, singles sometimes ask, When is a date not a date?

A date is not a date when a male and female are together but they have not made an appointment for the mutual enjoyment of some social activity or when neither one is romantically interested in the other. However, it is wise for a guy to make a practice of paying for the food and activities of the woman accompanying him, even when they're not on a date. By doing so he is better able to consider the financial obligations he will face if he ever chooses to marry. Far too many men enter marriage without that understanding.

Know That You Never Have to Date

There are several reasons why dating is a great idea. However, a person is not weird because he or she doesn't date. Jesus Christ didn't date, and He wasn't weird. I know many Christian married couples who never dated. They simply met, grew to know each other and married. Dating is not essential to a good marriage.

One young woman told me, "I've been asked to marry someone several times — by my parents!" Parent pressure, peer pressure, self-inflicted pressure can all make it appear as if marriage is the only way to happiness. Such pressure can push a person into a desperate panic. Dating becomes absolutely necessary to them, as they see dating as the only possible road to marriage. People living in such frustration will often accept dates with anyone. They may think irrationally:

If I have to sleep with him or her — or tell a few lies — at least he or she will marry me.

One of the most unkind comments anyone can make to a single person is, You mean you don't have a date? The inference is, If you were at all sharp, you'd have one. But many people who don't have a date need to thank God for His grace. One young woman complained to the Lord that no one was asking her out. She ended up begging God for a date. Finally a guy at work asked her out. He was handsome and had a great personality. As far as she knew, he was a Christian. On the third date he took her to his apartment and attempted date rape.

She told me, "I fought him, literally wrestling on his living room floor for ten minutes. I cried and pleaded with him to let me go. Finally I got a kick to his groin, and while he doubled up, I ran out of his apartment. I ran all the way to my house — five miles. I hadn't run more than a few steps in years. After bolting the door, I fell onto my living room sofa and cried for an hour. I had to have a girlfriend with me in my apartment for more than a month after that. I was so scared he'd get me. I was all bruises for a month too. Praise God, he's never spoken to me from that day to this. But I still have nightmares about him. Dating just anybody isn't what it's cracked up to be."

Dating people whose lives aren't committed to Christ never will be what it's cracked up to be. God had been protecting the woman in the above story. But she hadn't appreciated His protection. Now she does, and she knows that no date is better than the wrong date.

Someone may say, But all my friends are dating. Well, if they're not dating Christ-centered Christians, I predict a very unhappy future for most of them.

What should you be doing while you see all your friends dating?

> Wait for the Lord;
>   Be strong, and let your heart take courage;
> Yes, wait for the Lord.
>
> Psalm 27:14

You don't have to date.

Whom Should You Date?

Because a date means something, a single person needs to be extremely careful about whom he or she dates. Christian singles need to be especially careful, as their hearts (which belong to Jesus Christ) are suddenly being opened to the possibility of love with another human. Look at 2 Corinthians 6:14-15: "Do not be bound together with unbelievers; for what partnership have righteousness and

64

lawlessness, or what fellowship has light with darkness? Or what harmony has Christ with Belial, or what has a believer in common with an unbeliever?" This is often used to teach against marrying an unbeliever. But the passage goes deeper. Among other things, it is saying this: *Never date an unbeliever*. Perhaps the biggest question you as a Christian single will ever have to answer to God is, Do you want to date or get married more than you want the will of God for your life?

Who is an unbeliever? The word *unbeliever* and *unbelief* are used two ways in the New Testament. Obviously, an unbeliever is one who doesn't believe someone or something. So *unbeliever* is sometimes used to describe those who have never received Christ as Savior (Luke 12:46; Rev. 21:8). But *unbelief* is often used to describe someone who is not trusting Christ in a certain area of life and is resisting Him in that area (Mark 6:6; 1 Tim. 1:13). It doesn't mean such a person will never be born again. It might even describe what some call a backslider (one who is saved but has, for whatever reason, given him or herself momentarily to sin).

The Christian who seeks a romantic relationship with an unbeliever or the unsaved is flagrantly violating 2 Corinthians 6:14-7:1. In fact, 2 Corinthians 6:17 is a direct command from the Lord to "come out from their midst and be separate.... Do not touch what is unclean." Anyone attempting to unite in relationship with one who does not know Christ is in great peril of becoming unclean too.

One reason Christians are never to become "unequally yoked" is because "a natural man [unsaved person] does not accept the things of the Spirit of God; for they are foolishness to him, and he cannot understand them, because they are spiritually appraised" (1 Cor. 2:14). A romantic relationship with an unsaved person is both foolish and spiritually dangerous.

The big question is: "What has a believer in common with an unbeliever?" (2 Cor. 6:15). Tragically, as more and more churchgoers dilute their Christian testimony by attending the same movies, watching the same television shows, reading the same books and magazines, listening to the same music (and so forth) as do unbelievers, the answer seems to be: Well, we have almost everything in common. But that's not the answer God expects.

Though Christians should avoid dating unbelievers, there is one far more dangerous to be avoided: he or she who claims to be saved yet lives like an unbeliever (1 Cor. 5:9-13).

These singles attend church to play the dating game. They are the ones with the morals of an alley cat. They may know how to quote Scripture to impress, but they seldom live what they quote. I have even seen this kind of person on a church staff. Far more often, though, they're attending just long enough to find someone who wants human love more than God.

One frequent date scenario I see is a male (sometimes a female) who gets "saved" just to impress a member of the opposite sex. Yet any real observation of this "new convert" will show that old things didn't pass away; behold, hardly anything became new (2 Cor. 5:17). Outside church and away from those he or she wants to impress, this person isn't changed.

> A person who is pure of heart sees goodness and purity in everything; but a person whose own heart is evil and untrusting finds evil in everything, for his dirty mind and rebellious heart color all he sees and hears. Such persons claim they know God, but from seeing the way they act, one knows they don't. They are rotten and disobedient, worthless so far as doing anything good is concerned (Titus 1:15-16, LB).

Know anyone like that? Don't date him or her. "Do not be deceived: 'Bad company corrupts good morals' " (1 Cor. 15:33).

The devil wears many hats. He is "the father of lies" (John 8:44). He'd just as soon pretend to be a religious person, even a pastor or a priest, as he would a serpent. That's why you've got to know the Christ-centeredness of the one you date.

Talk is cheap. I recently heard a parrot that had been trained to say, "I am saved. I am saved." I don't believe the parrot!

In Mark 1:24 a demon in a man addressed Jesus, "I know who You are — the Holy One of God!" Jesus cast that demon out. Anyone can say he or she is saved or knows who Jesus is. But salvation requires a Christian life-style. Short of such a life-style, grace becomes disgrace and a sick joke.

Nearly every week Christian wives come to me crying, "My husband won't pray with me." Or "My husband refuses to go to church at all." In nearly all of these cases the wives wish they'd never dated these men, even if it meant being single for life.

Men also come to me in pain because their wives aren't Christians. They say things like, "My wife won't come to church, pray, read the Bible or do anything else with me." Or "She stays out late at night, and when she comes home, she says, 'Just trust your Jesus about where I've been.' "

These statements aren't extremes. Reports of incest, sexual unfaithfulness, alcoholism, drug addiction, physical abuse, crime and other sins listed in Romans 1:26-31 are far too common. Nearly all this heartache could have been avoided if people had made wise choices when they started dating.

Someone may say, But all my Christian friends are marrying unsaved people, and they seem very happy. Hebrews 11:25 warns of "the passing pleasures of sin." In other words, the pleasures of sin will pass, and "the wages of sin" (Rom. 6:23) will have to be paid.

Make a list right now of all your friends who have married unsaved people. Keep the list handy. Give these people ten years (in most cases it will be fewer). Then draw a line through the couples who have divorced. When you learn of each divorce, ask your divorced friend why it happened. Get ready to hear some horror stories. Many of them will make television soap operas seem dull.

Some may think that by ruling out both unbelievers and the singles they know who act like unbelievers, there would be no one left.

If there were really no believers available, they'd be better off staying single and never dating anyone. More to the point, a complaint that no Christ-centered singles exist is like Elijah crying to God that there were *no* godly people among the Israelites. God quickly opened Elijah's eyes to seven thousand he hadn't noticed (1 Kin. 19:13-18; Rom. 11:2-4). Pray and look around!

Why Date?

You should always be able to give God and yourself a good reason (or reasons) for why you are dating someone. Be honest about it. Follow this simple rule: I will always keep pure motives for dating.

What are some impure motives? Never date simply to impress someone else that you are datable or desirable. Never date because you covet or hope to steal someone else's boyfriend or girlfriend (Rom. 13:9-10). Dating to have sex with someone is ungodly (Col. 3:5-6). Dating the boss to get a promotion or raise or dating a woman because she's considered gorgeous by your friends is dating with impure motives.

Following are some pure reasons for dating. Keep them in mind.

1. *Date to develop friendships.* If you really want to get along in this world, it's important to get to know members of the opposite sex. One of the finest ways to learn what makes other people tick is to spend time alone with them. Dating gives you that opportunity.

Some argue that dating affords a couple so much physical temptation that it is too risky for Christians. But Christians have the fruit of self-control (Gal. 5:22-23). Dating requires no physical involvement at all.

2. *Date to have fun.* One major reason Jesus Christ came was to give us an "abundant life" (John 10:10). Once you get over the awkward feelings that often accompany first dates, you will usually find that dating is fun.

Predictions for the future include "dating contracts" to state legal rights and financial compensation from the guilty partner if either dater gets a venereal disease. The male would also have to pay all costs for any female who gets pregnant or wants an abortion because of him. In fact, such "insurance" would demand a large sum of money from whoever terminates the relationship. Brokerage firms would exist for the sole purpose of legalizing such contracts.

These trappings are preposterous. If you're not dating to have fun, you're dating for the wrong reasons.

3. *Date to feel good about yourself.* One of the silliest arguments raging among Christian teachers is whether or not a Christian should have high self-esteem. One day when a lawyer asked Christ what the most important law was, Jesus answered, " 'You shall love the Lord your God with all your heart, and with all your soul, and with all your mind.' This is the great and foremost commandment" (Matt. 22:37-38). That answer from Jesus ends all arguments about who is to be placed first in our lives.

But Jesus didn't stop there. Though the lawyer asked for the one highest commandment, Jesus threw in a freebie. He said, "The second is like it, 'You shall love your neighbor as yourself' " (Matt. 22:39). Think about that statement. If many people loved their neighbor as they love themselves, they'd hate their neighbor! I constantly counsel women and men with low self-esteem. They are mocked and ridiculed and have no sense of their own worth in Christ. The devil loves telling them how "worthless" they are. It keeps them from witnessing verbally, and it makes their Christian life so unattractive that no one would want a life like theirs. They live in constant fear of people and forever feel put down. If they do dare to date, they often become vulnerable targets for anyone who wants to take advantage of them.

The balance in the love-God, love-self commandments is underscored by Romans 12:3: "For through the grace given to me I say to every man [member of mankind] among you not to think more highly of [yourself] than [you] ought to think; but to think so as to have sound judgment, as God has allotted to each a measure of faith." No conceit, no selfishness. No room to say, God understands how weak I am, so this sin I'm committing is OK. *That's* "thinking more highly of yourself than you ought." Jesus Christ isn't your buddy. He is Lord.

But the Bible never says you're chopped liver. The message is just the opposite. "Or do you not know that your body is a temple of the Holy Spirit who is in you, whom you have from God, and that you are not your own? For you have been bought with a price: therefore glorify God in your body" (1 Cor. 6:19-20). Your body has high worth. It's not to be given away lightly. It's not to be used.

4. *Date to develop understanding.* Getting to know the opposite sex is one thing; learning to understand them is another. In *Marriage Plus* I devoted two chapters to the seven major differences between men and women (chapters 4 and 5). Do you know why most women prefer to talk much longer than most men do? Do you know why most women seem to know something intuitively long before men discover it? Do you know why most women have better long-term memories than most men? Do you know why most men are physically stronger than most

68

women? Look in *Marriage Plus*.

I highly recommend the Heinz 57 brand of dating, or at least the Baskin-Robbins 31. When you date several people and don't get serious with any, you keep a clearer mind, learn much more and begin to recognize the qualities needed in a person you'll consider marrying.

Some woman reading this may say, Are you kidding? I never — or rarely — get asked out on a date. But let me ask, How much time have you spent praying about this? Perhaps that kind of praying has seemed selfish or frivolous to you. But if you're hurting right now because you aren't dating, God cares. Tell Him.

At Singles Plus seminars I always recommend a remedy for the above situation: Schedule a Sadie Hawkins Day in your church singles' group the first Saturday of every fourth month. For that event the girls ask the guys, giving the women the opportunity to get to know someone they admire and would like to know better. Date-aggressive females tend to scare away most guys, so every four months is often enough.

5. *Date to learn to share.* Dating is a great way to learn to share time with someone else. Dating is one of the best teachers for learning how not to offend, how to give, how to enjoy life together and how to reach beyond yourself and your own interests.

6. *Date to "get out of your shell."* Sometimes the one who doesn't date isn't a workaholic or a hermit. He or she is shy and fearful. Willie and Willimina Wallflower need to change their ways, or they'll seldom find their lives fulfilling — to themselves or anybody else.

Becoming a turtle and pulling your head into your shell teaches you nothing. I hear plenty of reasons why people don't date: the possibility for emotional pain...too much sexual temptation...too much financial expense. These may well be obstacles to dating, but we as Christians are to be overcomers (Rev. 3:5,21; 12:11; 21:7) and not so afraid of life that we refuse to live it. When Christ is leading you, you can do all things in His power, not in your own. As Paul said, "I can do all things through Him who strengthens me" (Phil. 4:13).

Basic Rules of Consideration

Any person on any date can expect to be treated with kindness and consideration.

What does it mean to be treated with consideration? It means he shows he cares about you, ma'am, by arriving on time for dates; coming to the door and greeting family or anyone else; keeping his car clean; opening the car door — or any door — for you when you get in or out; dressing nicely so that you won't be uncomfortable to be seen with him; entering into real communication with you whether in person, by phone or by letter. It means he has good manners, and you aren't embarrassed or forced to apologize for him to your friends. It means he treasures you and shows it, never treating you like leftovers. It means you can trust him morally and that he doesn't have to play touchy-feely games to express his love.

Guys, know the difference between the words *casual* and *dressy*, and tell your date, at least three days in advance, which way she should dress for the outing (unless it's obvious). If you are going bowling or on a hayride, the attire should be casual, even very casual. If you are going to a concert or play, she'll most likely dress "dressy" or even very dressy. Nearly all women feel out of place when dressed inappropriately.

What does it mean for you, sir, to be treated with consideration? It means she shows she cares about you by being ready when you arrive to pick her up. She keeps her living quarters comfortable but not cluttered (because that's almost for certain how she'll keep her house after marriage); she keeps her car clean; she says thank you when you open car doors or do something thoughtful for her; she dresses nicely so that you won't be uncomfortable to be seen with her. It means she uses good manners, and her actions don't make you have to "explain her" to any of your friends. It means she shows she's delighted to be with you and tells you so. It means you can trust her morally and that she doesn't tease you physically or by how she dresses.

Enthusiastic consideration for another person is as contagious as the measles.

Be Creative

With Christ in the center of the party, a date should be fun. My son David is what I call a creative dater. Imagine the joy of his date (a ballerina) when he took her to the Bolshoi ballet in Los Angeles. But once he'd bought those tickets, David knew he couldn't afford to take her to a restaurant first. So he made other plans. He told her how she was to dress (dressy) and what time he was picking her up, but he gave no other details. A few days before the date he requisitioned a small and attractive room at the church where he worked. (The room even had a stained-glass window.) The afternoon of the date, David prepared a special meal, including cheese fondue and strawberry shortcake (a favorite of hers). At the church he set the scene: lace tablecloth, china, crystal, candles and lovely music via tape recorder. When he picked up his date, he drove her to the church ("to do something very important"). When they arrived, he asked her to come in because a co-worker wanted to see how beautiful she looked. The rest was a thrilling surprise.

Dates never have to be as expensive as the Bolshoi ballet, but they are most fun when they are creative. Not every date will be as elaborate or fully planned as David's. But a steady diet of watching movies or TV runs the risk of becoming boring and is not healthy to a relationship. Think of the possibilities: bowling, Ping-Pong, tennis, golf, a sports event, a concert or play, a drive, eating out, fishing, Monopoly, Scrabble, Big Boggle or any favorite game (mine is Balderdash), a walk, a bicycle or horseback ride, yardwork or a house project, a picnic — all can be relatively inexpensive ways of having a blast. Some of them won't cost you anything but a happy time.

If you're looking for new ideas for dating, read *Creative Dating* and *More Creative Dating* by Doug Fields and Todd Temple (Oliver Nelson Publishing). They'll keep you laughing and help you become far more interesting.

The idea that dates cost too much comes from people who haven't been thinking creatively or from the misguided who honestly believe a date that costs nothing is worth nothing. Many college girls complain to me that "the guys do not ask the girls out." Reason? The guys think they won't have enough money to pay for the dates. Should the girls pay instead? No — or they will pay for it as long as the relationship lasts. Instead, both the guys and the girls need to settle for inexpensive or no-cost dates. Girls, don't sit and mope because Prince Charming never comes calling with a glass slipper. Have a ball!

Guys, when dating, take the lead. It can bug a woman to have a guy pick her up for a date and then ask, "Where would you like to go?" True, he may feel he's giving her the right to choose. But her feeling might be, Don't you know what you're doing? After a few dates he will be able to determine the kinds of places she'd most like to go to (because he has learned about her interests). He'll still keep his own interests in mind too, because, should they ever marry, they'll need to share each other's interests. If you are dating a woman for the first time and have two equally worthwhile places in mind, you might phone her ahead of time and ask which she'd prefer.

A Serious Promise

Hebrews 13:4 defines God's word on who may have sex. "Let marriage be held in honor among all, and let the marriage bed be undefiled; for fornicators and adulterers God will judge." (*Judge* in this verse is *krino* in the original Greek text and means "to condemn to hell.") Fornicators are unmarried persons engaging in sexual intercourse. Adulterers are married persons who have sex with anyone other than their spouses. No one has a right to have sex outside of marriage.

God has preserved sex only for marriage — a heterosexual relationship that is sealed with a lifetime commitment.

America is a nation full of people screaming for their "rights." After speaking to a college group, I was accosted by an angry student: "I didn't like what you shared. You make it sound like everybody's got to go to heaven."

Without thinking how it would come across, I answered, "No, you can go to hell if you want to."

Ultimately, the only right you have in this whole world is to decide for yourself whether you want to go to heaven or to hell. You will go to one of those two places when you die. All humans will. Paul says "your spiritual service of worship" has most to do with making your body "a living and holy sacrifice" to God (Rom. 12:1). Surrender what this world says is your right to free sex.

Inwardly make this promise to every person you date: I promise God and you that I am willing never to be married. I will care about you, but I won't force you to marry me, and I won't have sex with you unless we are married to each other.

You cannot break God's rules without ultimately getting your heart broken.

Chapter 10 gives a more complete discussion of sexual issues and temptation. Stay with me until you read that chapter.

Loose conduct can quickly get you
into tight places.

Questions for Reflection and Discussion

1. Write an answer to the letter that precedes chapter 3. Carefully answer each of the four questions she asks.

2. Carefully study 2 Corinthians 6:14-15. What do these verses have to do with dating an unbeliever? What is the difference between someone who calls himself a Christian and someone who is a real believer? Is the difference always immediately apparent? (See Galatians 5:19-24 for a contrast.) Write down a clear definition of "believer" and "unbeliever." What implications do these definitions have in the instructions Paul gives in 1 Corinthians 7:12-16?

3. What does the word "date" mean to you? Is there a difference between dating someone or simply going out as friends? In either case, why is it so important to keep 1 Corinthians 15:33 in mind? Why do you think that God places so much emphasis on being separate from the world, yet being the "salt of the earth" (Matt. 5:13) to those around you? On a practical basis, how can this be done?

4. In marriage God assigns the husband to be "the provider" for the family's needs (1 Tim. 5:8). How important do you believe it is for the male to get used to this by paying all dating expenses? Should there be any exceptions to this? If he pays for the date, is the female obligated to do anything physical to "thank him" for the date? Discuss this thoroughly.

5. Some Christian singles feel they have the right to use their bodies as they please and that God will "understand" the sexual pressures they face. Carefully study 1 Corinthians 6:13b-20 in the Amplified Bible. What does it mean to be "united to the Lord (become one spirit)"? Why do you feel that God holds Christians to such high (according to the world) sexual standards? Write down what you find and then discuss it.

Dear Ray,

I'm feeling the kind of pain no pain-killer will stop. My husband is gone. He just walked out one day and left me with one little baby who took "too much of his time." My son is five now and still takes a lot of time. I heard you speak at a one-day conference, and I enjoyed what you shared. But it hurt when you said, "God will meet your deepest needs," quoting powerful Scripture to back up your claim. It hurts because I feel abandoned, totally rejected, by my husband, but also by God.

If Jesus came to bring us "life more abundant," how come my life stinks? I am home with my son or out at a restaurant where I work all the time. I meet guys, even Christian guys, who talk nice and seem great. Several guys have asked me out. I always turn them down. I do it because I don't know what God thinks about a divorced woman dating. So I'm writing to ask you what God thinks about it. Should I date? What would it do for me? Am I more likely to find "life more abundant" if I date or don't date?

Lonely and Wanting to Do God's Will

*The thief comes only to steal,
and kill, and destroy;
I came that they might have life,
and might have it abundantly.*

John 10:10

FOUR

WHAT ABOUT
MY SPECIAL CASE?

Many people are lonely because
they build walls instcad of bridges.

Widows, widowers, divorced persons and single parents often ask whether or not they should consider dating and remarriage. Let's look at the special concerns of these three groups.

Should a Widowed Person Date?

First, no widow or widower ever *has to* date. A deep grief period of one to two years after losing a spouse is normal. To some who have become widowed, the thought of dating again would be unappealing. But sometimes those who had a happy marriage find they don't like living alone. They do want to date and marry again. Since dates don't have to include any physical contact, not even a kiss, there is no reason why widowed persons need to cut themselves off from the opposite sex. Life for the living here on earth should continue.

I'm sometimes asked if dating or remarrying isn't being disloyal to a deceased spouse. Might it hurt the feelings of the departed? Jesus Christ seems to have answered both questions in Matthew 22:25-30. First, He reveals no problem with a widow (who has outlived six husbands) marrying for a seventh time. Second, He says, "For in the resurrection they neither marry, nor are given in marriage, but are like angels in heaven" (v. 30). Christians always want God's best for everyone. Certainly "when this perishable will have put on the imperishable, and this mortal will have put on immortality, then will come about the saying that is written, 'Death is swallowed up in victory' " (1 Cor. 15:54). Jealousy, and all other sin, is nonexistent in the Christian dead who have gone ahead of us.

There is, however, reason for some caution in dating. A widow or widower, lonely and in grief, can become the victim of an unscrupulous person who is interested in "marrying money." A person with much wealth or property needs to be aware of this and use sound judgment. All courting couples of any age should always seek godly, totally honest counsel before marrying. When an older person is being courted (especially by someone quite a bit younger), this is even more crucial. They must ask of their counselor: Based on all you know about me and this other person, do you think we should marry? They must then listen very carefully to their answer. They must not let their hearts rule their heads. If the counsel is against marrying the person, the one receiving the counsel will be wise to follow it. If you are in the position of answering such a question, give an honest answer.

Another factor remains: A second marriage *is* a second marriage. Inevitably there will be comparisons made between a first husband or wife and the second spouse. As one second husband told me, "Jesus Christ wasn't the only perfect man in history. My wife says her first husband was perfect too!" While one in two marriages in America is now ending in divorce, the odds for happiness in any subsequent marriage are poor.

Should a Divorced Person Date?

There are an average of one million remarriages in America every year. The National Center for Health Statistics says that more than 70 percent of divorced people (83 percent of the men and 78 percent of the women) will remarry. About one-third of *all* Americans will marry at least twice. According to research at

Northwestern University, by the mid-1990s the stepfamily will be the most common family type in the United States. But nearly 50 percent of these families will break up within the first five years after the remarriage.

To quote from *U.S. News and World Report*, "Newly remarried couples face from three to ten times the stress — including financial, relocation, the tensions of step-parenting and dealing with former spouses — as do those in first marriages." Whether a second marriage will succeed has to do with two things: (1) how close the single person considering remarriage is in his or her walk with Christ and (2) how careful this person is to date only those who have that same kind of walk.

No one should ever date anyone (except his or her spouse) while married or divorcing. If a person going through a divorce isn't in grief over the tragedy of one being torn in two (Mark 10:8), there is reason to ask why. A person divorcing while having in view another love partner is in sin. Such a person has not understood the great sanctity in which God holds marriage. Jesus Christ said, "What therefore God hath joined together, let not man [or woman] put asunder" (Mark 10:9, KJV).

For the first twelve years of my marriage, I reasoned that God surely wouldn't hold me responsible for a "tiny mistake" I'd made when I was twenty-two. I told Him, "Look, Lord, I was just a kid when I got married. You wouldn't blame me if I erased my tiny mistake, would You, by getting a divorce?"

God stayed silent. He never has to speak when His Bible already does. The Bible spoke *loudly*. The Lord said:

> "And this is another thing you do: you cover the altar of the Lord with tears, with weeping and with groaning, because He no longer regards the offering or accepts it with favor from your hand. Yet you say, 'For what reason?' Because the Lord has been a witness between you and the wife of your youth, against whom you have dealt treacherously, though she is your companion and your wife by covenant. But not one has done so who has a remnant of the Spirit.... Take heed then, to your spirit, and let no one deal treacherously against the wife of your youth. For I hate divorce" (Mal. 2:13-16).

Jesus said, "Everyone who divorces his wife, except for the cause of [*porneia*], makes her commit adultery; and whoever marries a divorced woman commits adultery" (Matt. 5:32). The Greek word *porneia* literally means "a spirit of whoredom." Neither my wife nor I had committed unrepented sexual sin. Incompatibility is never biblical grounds for divorce.

Any counselor who shoves the Bible aside and expects God to wink at sexual sin or easy divorce to make people comfortable is an ungodly counselor. Allowing sexual sin or ignoring what God has to say on divorce may make someone feel good for a moment. But it is like making a cancer in someone's body comfortable. It ultimately will kill them.

There *are* biblical exceptions that allow for divorce under certain hideous situations (Matt. 5:31-32; 1 Corin. 7:15-16). God never gives *license* for divorce. Divorce should be considered as a possibility only when a spouse has been deserted or when sin is so heavily destructive to the believer or offspring that continuation of it could cause irreparable emotional damage, physical harm or death. Even then I have seen so many miracles during Marriage Plus seminars that the Goliath of divorce has no chance against the rock of God's Word (Matt. 7:24-27). "For nothing will be impossible with God" (Luke 1:37).

In evaluating every divorced couple's situation, there is nearly always the one who caused the divorce (by violating the marriage covenant) and the victim (the one who tried everything he or she knew to make the marriage a success). If you had a divorce and are honest about what caused it, you'll know in which category you fit.

The covenant-breaker who by action makes divorce inevitable is in great trouble with God (Mal. 2:13-16; Heb. 10:28-31). One can only hope such a person will cry out for the mercy and cleansing of God (1 John 1:9-10). Until such a time, a sinner will tend to repeat the sin. Though this person should date no one, he or she wouldn't care what God requires. The only good news is that when Christians pray for covenant-breakers, like prodigal sons or daughters, the sinners have a great talent for galloping into pigpens and waking up (Luke 15:14-19).

To the victim of divorce whose spouse is the covenant-breaker, dating is as available as it is to the widowed. Of course, a divorced person may choose never to date again. If that choice isn't motivated by unrepentant bitterness, the divorced person may stay happily single for the rest of his or her life.

The man paying alimony may not be able to afford to date. Alimony is like paying for a car after it's been totaled — but it costs a whole lot more. Alimony *must* be paid. The Christian who complains about paying alimony should be the first to understand the importance of this book: Choosing a life partner must be done with total care and total prayer. The whole married life has to be handled the very same way. Alimony is the cost of *not* doing that. One ex-husband told me, "You never know what a wife is worth until you start paying alimony!"

The finest book I've read on the biblical view of divorce is Jay E. Adams's *Marriage, Divorce and Remarriage* (Baker Book House). My message "The Truth About Divorce" may be helpful and is available on cassette.

Should a Single Parent Date?

From 1970 to 1983 the number of one-parent families with children increased by 107 percent, while two-parent families decreased by 5 percent. There are more than twelve million single parents in America, more than half of them with children under age eighteen. And the predicted rate of increase in single parenting is 33 percent. If you are a single parent, you are not alone.

One can be a single parent for any number of reasons. Widowed. Divorced. Many singles give birth out of wedlock.

I warmly thank all unwed mothers who have chosen to keep their babies or allowed them to be adopted into loving families rather than choosing abortion. God has a great purpose for your child (or children). If they were born because of moral failure at an earlier moment in your life, know that the blood of Jesus Christ is sufficient to cleanse you from *all* sin (1 John 1:9). Take advantage of Christian counseling. Be sure you have dealt with the problems that led to your fall. If your child is living with you, he or she will observe you through the years; your actions must glorify the Lord and remain pure.

I'm often asked by single parents, "At what point should I let a prospective date know I have a child?" My advice is to make this clear, as a part of normal conversation, before you ever accept a date. Don't apologize or act as if the information will surely cancel the possibility of dating. Answer questions honestly. If someone backs off from dating you because you are a parent, he or she eventually would have backed off anyway. Boot not to begin a dating relationship that has no future but heartbreak.

Any person you date is a potential stepparent of your children. Does your date care for them? It can't be stressed enough that dating in itself requires a maturity that cannot be neglected without great danger.

One of the saddest reports I hear from both men and women in second marriages is, "My spouse is mean to my kids." I always wonder how that second spouse was able to bluff his or her way into marriage, keeping the prospective spouse from knowing he or she would be mean. Second marriages can create hard times for all of the family.

Saying "I love you" to someone who is also a mother or father must mean, "I fully accept any child who has come from you." The parent who is remarrying must be able to say, "I trust you to love my offspring and help me 'train [them] up...in the way [they] should go' " (Prov. 22:6). In a Christian home where a single parent has raised a child or children, a second marriage requires both the husband and wife to do everything within their power to show loving care and offer security to the whole family.

Time is the greatest gift any parent will ever give to a child. Single parents often feel guilty because they simply don't have all the time their children demand of them. Remember, you can be a mom or a dad, but not both. For continual bonding, your child needs daily time wherein you can give spiritual input (Bible study, prayer, and the like) and simply communicate (talking, laughing together, sharing some housework or gardening or other project). These things cannot be shoved aside for dating without risking a deep breach in your parent-child relationship.

For various reasons some single parents decide not to date. Some are so busy parenting and earning a living that they have no time or energy left to date. However, the happiest single parents I've met tell me they have worked out a healthy balance that includes time with their youngsters and needed "break" times when they seek the fellowship of other adults. Dating is often a part of this break.

A night or two out each week for the parent might work well. Younger children (until early teens) will require a Christian baby-sitter who can be trusted and whom the children like. Older teenagers usually have activities that keep them busy one or two nights a week.

Children or teenagers who see their parent dating someone other than their real mother or father may feel confusion, anger, fear, jealousy and a whole gamut of other negative emotions toward both the custodial parent and the date. They've been abandoned by one parent. So anyone the custodial parent dates is a real risk to them; they may "lose" this parent to the other person. It isn't unusual for a child or teenager to express hateful feelings under such circumstances. As a parent, do not ignore this and let your children lock themselves into a state of doom and gloom (2 Cor. 10:5b). If you do, the established habit may last a lifetime. Keep reassuring your children that you love them; even if you were to marry this other person, you would not love them any less. If you see that your conversation is going nowhere and that they still hold their anger, have them talk with their pastor or youth director or a professional counselor who loves Christ and may be able to bring emotional relief.

What you do or allow with any date will make an impression on your children, who will feel they have every right to do the same things when they begin to date. You are their role model. Be able to say to your offspring, "Be imitators of me, just as I also am of Christ" (1 Cor. 11:1).

It can't be emphasized enough that when Christ forgives and cleanses a sinner, He washes away their sin (1 John 1:9). Former sinners become as if they had never sinned. So a parent who had a baby without marriage should never feel like a hypocrite when setting down rules that will keep the child or teenager from immorality. There will usually come moments, especially when the child is in the teen years, when a mother or father who was once involved in immorality and is now cleansed can talk of the pain and emotional suffering that accompanies sexual sin. This is seldom easy. It should not be casual or constant. But it can help the young person understand why sexual immorality is never worth it.

The church is an essential part of every Christian's life. If you are a single parent, talk with your pastor and find out what can be done to minister to your child's need for a missing dad or mom. The church that is aware of its need to provide godly role models (that is, a Christian man who will take your son or daughter fishing or to a ball game or a godly woman who will take your daughter or son shopping or to a museum) can help your offspring develop an emotional balance that includes both men and women. Obviously, the church must know the moral character of those who are used for such a ministry, but I recommend a "big brother" or "big sister" group for every church.

There is a magnificent promise given to every single parent. It's the same promise I've lived by for more than twenty years when I've had to be away from my wife for weeks at a time. Proverbs 3:5-6:

> Trust in the Lord with all your heart,
>   And do not lean on your own understanding.
> In all your ways acknowledge Him,
>   And He will make your paths straight.

To master temptation, let Christ master you.

Questions for Reflection and Discussion

1. Write an answer to the letter preceding chapter 4. Should she date?

2. Is it right that God should "hate divorce" (Mal. 2:16)? How serious is divorce? How many people does a churchgoer's divorce affect? Write down all the repercussions you can think of that come as a direct result of a couple divorcing. Discuss this list thoroughly.

3. Discuss the pros and cons of a widowed person dating. Should a divorced person date? Should a single parent date? What does God's Word say about this?

4. What role, if any, should the church play in encouraging fellowship among single parents, the widowed or divorced? Is there a difference between encouraging "fellowship" and encouraging "dating"?

5. List ways single parents could help their children or teenagers accept the parents' desire to date and to accept their dates. What should be done? What should never be done? Discuss your list.

Dear Ray,

   As a college professor teaching a life studies course at a Christian college, I'm writing you for some specific information. Nearly all of my students date. I want to do a section on that subject. What should I tell my students about dating? What guidelines could you share with us?
   The few who don't date are generally shy and need help in that regard. What guidelines could you give these few to help them form friend relationships?

   A Professor Who Cares About the Lives of His Students

*Two are better than one
because they have a good return
for their labor.
For if either of them falls,
the one will lift up his companion.
But woe to the one who falls
when there is not another
to lift him up.*

Ecclesiastes 4:9-10

FIVE

HOW TO MAKE YOURSELF ATTRACTIVE TO OTHERS

Develop character — don't be one!

I learned early in life that bribery doesn't get you friends. By the time I reached puberty I was carrying the weight of the world's best cooking. Short and fat, I had few friends and *no* girlfriends. Meanwhile, I was attending a school full of daters. Much of the loneliness I carried into early adulthood was picked up in elementary and high school when I looked more like a Mardi Gras balloon than a human. I felt the inner pain of every pound I carried. Kids can be very mean when they decide someone doesn't fit in their social order. I didn't fit, so I tried to buy friends with the nickels Mom gave me for my lunch money.

I would go to Lucky Creamery, the sandwich shop across from my school, but I didn't buy anything for myself. A gang of the kids from my class would all be huddled together, laughing and having a good time. I'd wait for my chance. Finally, as the crowd dispersed, I'd ask, "Would anybody like a Coke?" Several would always say yes. I'd take them to the Coke machine outside the restaurant and, like a rich man, pump nickels into the slot. Each kid would light up and say, "Thanks," as I'd hand him or her a cold bottle. When all my nickels were gone, they'd wander off together, leaving me. I ached for the attention of any one of the girls carrying my Cokes. But, no, their attentions were gone before the drinks were swallowed.

Neither friendship nor a true romance can be bought. Sooner or later there is always a higher bidder. But there are ways you can draw people to you. Some people who want to date (but do not) don't realize how easily they could make people more at ease in their company. Here are some tips for making yourself attractive to others.

Mind Your Manners

When I went to college and got away from home, I quickly forgot most of my manners. I would have told you at the time that I liked "relaxing" at mealtimes and saw no need to keep alert to what I was doing with my knife, fork and spoon. When Arlyne began dating me after graduation, she saw that my manners would not win me any prizes. So she made a major common mistake. She said nothing about my manners until *after* we were married. Then she tried to change my ways. I reacted as most husbands do when their wives try to change them. I got mad. I felt it was none of her business. (I was wrong. She was trying to love me enough to risk offending me so I wouldn't be a further embarrassment to her or myself.)

There *is* a set place for your water glass — so it won't interfere with other items on a table. A salad fork is for the salad, not for spaghetti and meatballs. One does need to chew and swallow food *before* trying to deliver the Gettysburg Address — or taking another bite. Soup should be seen and not heard.

Good manners are part of the key to loving families, to promotions and raises at work, to joy in dating and marriage and to being liked. Don't fight anyone who really knows and can help you learn good manners. Thank God for that person.

Grossing out your date will cost you dearly. Belching, picking your teeth or nose or scratching private parts of your body are definitely out. Personal hygiene is in. That means making good use of toothpaste, mouthwash, soap and deodorant. It means keeping your nails clean and trim. Dirt or stains on your clothing are turn-offs. Wearing something that carries a body odor is offensive.

Embarrassment caused by an unthinking date can ruin his or her chances for getting a subsequent date with that person. That doesn't mean anyone dating should have to walk on eggshells, fearing he or she will do something wrong. It does mean everyone should know and practice being pleasant company. Good manners are an integral part of being good company.

To think that either dating or marriage will give you the right to be impolite so you can "relax" and "be yourself" is selfish ignorance. "Yourself" ought to be polite, relaxed or not. If you are a Christian, your witness for Christ should be the witness of a thoughtful, caring person. Manners are proof that you care about others, even when your mind is on something else. That's why manners have to be good habits and not just put on for company.

Cultivate a Positive Attitude and a Smile

It would take far more than one book to explain why you act the way you do. The Bible tells you what can be done to change for the better. By nature some people are more positive than others. Your parents, those who raised you, family, friends, teachers, television and the mass media all had their hand in making you what you are today. Your ancestors did, too.

None of the above truth gives you the "right" to blame any of them for your character weaknesses. Any normal human can develop the strengths of their personality type and let go of most of the weaknesses.

Positive people usually get positive results. Weeping over the past will seldom make a date anything but a bad experience. First-time daters who feel they should tell their dates every sad tale of their lives are usually last-time daters. This doesn't mean a dater should stay mute about something that fits in to a pleasant conversation, but, in general, Christians should be positive people. Even the tragedies in your life can ultimately cause good things to happen (Rom. 8:28). No matter how long you've been dating someone, when you tell him or her something sad or negative, bring Christ into your story. Relate how Christ has ministered to you and others in the particular situation. That will leave the person "up," rather than wanting to give you up.

The old adage "If you can't say something good, don't say anything at all" is a good one to live by, especially when dating. Tearing down any former dates will hurt you, not help you. The one you're dating will think, If he tears down his dates, what will he say about me to somebody else? But, on the other hand, sharing things you really liked about any former dates could make your date think, If that person was so great, why did they break up? I guess my date is still carrying a torch for that person. I probably won't measure up.

There are limits to positive thinking. No matter how positive your thoughts, you can't strike a match in a bowl of milk. It was one thing for Daniel to think positively while he was going into the lions' den, but God had to "think positively" for the lions (Dan. 6:3-22).

William Arthur Ward, writer-in-residence at Texas Wesleyan University in Fort Worth, gave a great definition of the difference between positive people and negative people. He said, "The pessimist complains about the gravel in his shoes; the optimist is grateful for shoes."[1] He then went on to give three timeless truths every single person should remember:

1. *Failure is not fatal.* Failure should be our teacher, not our undertaker. It should challenge us to new heights of accomplishment, not pull us to new depths of despair. Failure is a temporary detour, not a dead-end street. Remember, the greatest failure is the failure to try.

2. *Delays are not deadly.* Too often we equate delay with defeat. Frequently the best thing that can happen to us is a wise delay in our plans. If it's worth having, it's worth waiting for, and its value is often enhanced by delay. Delays are often God's way of teaching us the virtue of patience. And patience is more than a virtue; it is a required course in the school of life.

3. *Pressures are not permanent.* Problems and pressures do not stay. They are temporary and transitory, and they evaporate when we realize our internal resources are much stronger than the external pressures. Truly, greater is the power within you than any other power on earth (1 John 4:4).

If you haven't understood these three points until now, concentrate on them. Living by these principles will greatly help to keep you positive.

As for smiles, they are like bank loans. They always command interest. What's more, they reap rewards for you that go beyond winning friends. Psychologist Robert Baron explains, "If you smile, you feel happier, even if there is no reason to feel happy. If you frown, you get more upset. It has something to do with our facial muscles. Their movements do have a very important effect upon our internal state. If you're angry, and you grit your teeth, it only makes you angrier. But if you're scowling, and you make yourself grin, that really makes you feel better."[2] The Scriptures say the same: "A cheerful heart does good like medicine" (Prov. 17:22, LB).

When you make mountains out of molehills, don't expect anyone else to climb up and admire the view. Misery may love company, but it seldom gets any company worth having around. It surely doesn't draw the right kind of husband or wife.

Cultivate a Good Sense of Humor

Humor is also required for a great date life. Tension has a way of evaporating when people laugh with each other — not at each other.

Marriage Plus and Singles Plus seminars are full of funny jokes and one-liners. At the Singles Plus seminars I advise participants to know at least five clean, funny jokes for each date they go out on. They're great icebreakers when things quiet down. These jokes need to be sure-fire hits that would make anyone laugh. That means they shouldn't be ethnic slurs, distasteful, sick or offensive in any way.

Look on the funny side of life. Learn to laugh at yourself and the funny things you do.

A sense of humor is a necessary ingredient for strengthening relationships. Couples are more likely to stay together if they share a sense of humor. Humor can indicate many things: values, intelligence, interests, preoccupations, needs and imagination.

One other tip: You may think practical jokes are funny, but they are almost always impractical on a date. Those clowns who plant whoopie cushions or pull a date's chair out so far that she falls on the floor will probably spend a lot of lonely nights wondering why they are ignored. Again, never make anyone the brunt of your jokes.

As with the smile, there are health benefits to laughter. Research shows that when you have a hearty laugh, your metabolism picks up, your muscles get massaged and neurochemicals flow into your bloodstream. That means you've raised a strong guard against depression, stress, heart disease and pain.

Learn Good Communication Skills

Put your mind in gear before you put your mouth in motion. A mindless stream of words is not communication. *Communication* means "a stimulating conversation on both ends, but not an argument."

I hear complaints of why people don't go on second dates: "She didn't listen." "He did all the talking." "Every time I said anything, she just said 'uh-huh' and started talking about something completely off my point. She never even heard what I said."

To any single who finds it difficult to communicate, I recommend a Dale Carnegie course or a speech or drama class (to loosen up). You might have a friend help you role-play a dialogue with a date. The exercise will help you think of things to talk about with a date.

To facilitate conversation, find out as much as possible about a prospective date. In what city was he raised? What are her special interests? What sports, music or hobbies interest her? What are his plans for the future? As you explore these kinds of questions, you can find common interests and also learn something new. Remember that listening is at least half the secret of communication. James 1:19 says, "Let everyone be quick to hear, slow to speak...."

I hear other complaints about dates who can't communicate well: "He's so dull. He bored me." Or "She is so limited. She could talk about only one subject, nothing else."

One young woman told me, "All he wanted to do was kiss — because he couldn't think of a word to say. What a nerd!" Necking instead of communicating often means terrible communication problems if the couple marries; they've never learned to talk with each other.

Good grammar and correct pronunciation are a sign of intelligence. "Uh," "well," "you know" or mumbled, slurred speech are signs of poor communication skills that need to be corrected.

Don't Take God's Name in Vain or Swear

The National Institute of Business Management, which publishes the newsletter *Working Smart*, surveyed professional men and women (in secular fields) to find out what practices are unacceptable in the workplace. Eighty-three percent said they detested hearing sexual jokes; 69 percent said they were disgusted by hearing anyone swear. Few people will believe you're a Christian if you talk like the devil.

A major part of self-control is mouth-control. Cursing God brings you under His curse (Ex. 20:7; Deut 5:11). If swearing hurts God's ears, it surely ought to hurt yours. And if you're saying, "But all my friends swear," what does that say about the friends you've chosen?

Swearing embarrasses Christians. So don't embarrass your date.

Be Courteous

One of the deepest honors I have as a parent is that my kids trust me enough and have wanted to introduce my wife and me to those they date. I can honestly say I've never met one of their dates I didn't like. The date who is courteous, taking time to have friendly conversations with the parent(s) or friend(s), earns respect from everybody. When your date is relaxed and friendly with the important people in your life, you are impressed! You feel great when you hear others say how much they enjoyed meeting your date.

Flirting with anyone other than your date is out. But friendliness and a noncombative spirit with everyone (even the cashier who tries to shortchange you) are in. Arguing with anyone while on a date is a sure-fire way of making your date sorry he or she is with you.

Courteous drivers silently say, I care about your life. They drive defensively, not offensively. They don't want to offend the ones they're with. They'd rather be safe than sorry and keep their dates feeling the same way. They don't "peel rubber" — a juvenile act to get attention.

Avoid being melodramatic or a show-off on dates. A good rule of thumb is: Trying to impress will usually depress.

The courteous date says "thank you" whenever anyone does something nice. The courteous date says "I'm sorry" when he or she has done anything offensive, even if not directly at fault. A careful study of the Bible's love chapter, 1 Corinthians 13, especially verses 4-7, gives a deeper understanding of the way a date should act.

Be Tactful

Love is kind (1 Cor. 13:4).

Many people believe they have been personally appointed by God to rain on your parade. Make a mistake, and they'll put it on the six o'clock news. But before they publish the glad tidings, they will give you a piece of their mind.

On the other hand, there are those who know how to build you up when you're falling down. One of my favorite stories is of the guide who took a high government official on a pheasant hunt. That evening another official asked the guide, "How did my co-worker do at hunting birds today?" The tactful guide answered, "He shot most beautifully, but the Lord was very merciful to the birds."

Tact is the ability to pull the stinger out of the bee without getting stung!

Tact calls for a kindness that recognizes that "all have sinned and fall short of the glory of God" (Rom. 3:23). It's never glad about somebody else's misfortune. Instead, a tactful person is eager to follow God's directions in Galatians 6:1: "Brethren, even if a man is caught in any trespass, you who are spiritual, restore such a one in a spirit of gentleness; each one looking to yourself, lest you too be tempted." Gentleness (not wimpishness) is the first ingredient needed in helping someone who has sinned return to a full knowledge of Christ's love. (*Gentleness*, like meekness, means "great strength under God's control.")

Tactful people don't feel they have to tell their friends everything they know or feel. They care deeply, but they don't give advice too freely. They know they are not the Holy Spirit; unless they have a clear word from God that their friends can receive, they pray rather than bray.

I wince when I hear spouses attack each other with harsh words. Unkind statements making another person feel or look stupid prove the *speaker* is ignorant. Tactful people don't attack.

93

Be Trustworthy

One of my favorite funny songs is "Wake Up, Little Susie," recorded years ago by the Everly Brothers. It tells about a guy and his girlfriend who fall asleep at a drive-in theater. When they wake up at about 4 a.m., everybody else's car is gone; the film has been over for hours. They know they're in deep trouble, as they should have been home hours earlier. What is everybody going to think they were doing? What are her parents going to say? There's a classic line in the song: "Our reputation is shot."

Each of us has three names: the name inherited from ancestors, the name given by parents and the name we make for ourselves. We usually can't do much about the first two names. But we have nearly everything to do with the third. What do people say about you? What kind of reputation do you have? Do the people you've dated think of you as a moral person? a trustworthy person?

"Say just a simple 'Yes, I will' or 'No, I won't.' Your word is enough" (Matt. 5:37, LB).

Gene Brown tells the story of a college freshman football player who was interviewed by the coach from a big university. "Yes," said the student, "I can run one hundred yards in less than ten seconds, with full uniform. I block so well that last season four of our opponents had broken legs. As for passing, I can pass about sixty yards on the average — into the wind. As for my grades, I have always been on the dean's list." The coach was impressed.

"But, son," he said, "everyone has some weakness or deficiency. What's yours?"

"Well," said the candidate, "I'm inclined to lie a little."

Studies by University of Texas psychologists show that lying and cheating go hand in hand with low self-esteem. When people with low self-esteem begin to like themselves more, they are less apt to feel a need to be dishonest.

Someone has said, "No one has a good enough memory to rely on lying." Ever lie and then forget exactly what you'd said? As you stumble to keep every element in the lie believable, people begin to close in on you, and you are hung by your own noose! All excuses, alibis, explanations and apologies you fabricate on the spot or carefully create to cover your mistakes or sins (or those of somebody else) are lies.

Being trustworthy and being moral go hand in hand. Immoral people are thieves who steal fleshly treasures and run when they think a better treasure has come along. If you can't be trusted, don't date.

Don't Be Stingy

Give, and it will be given to you; good measure, pressed down, shaken together, running over, they will pour into your lap. For by your standard of measure it will be measured to you in return (Luke 6:38).

Selfishness short-circuits any kind of friendship. It takes. It doesn't give. Selfish persons want what they want when they want it. They live in their own kingdom called Instant Gratification and only let you in when you bring a gift they momentarily want. God's perfect timing, goals and plans all mean nothing to the selfish persons who believe they deserve a break today. The selfish are never dependable; they will share only when it's in their best interest. Reach out. Live for others, not yourself.

Inner Beauty

If after reading and heeding the tips in this chapter you still feel you're undatable, take encouragement from the words of the following woman and man who learned what to look for in a date.

The woman said, "They say that clothes make the man, but it's not true. Clothes improve a man's appearance, but it is still the Lord who makes the man. When a Christian single guy really lives the Christian life, he *is* attractive and a great person to date anytime. He can be trusted, so I can always be relaxed and feel safe. He knows where he's going, and, because he follows Christ, I want to go with him. Thank God for every single Christian male."

The man said, "I used to look at women and think they were all beautiful; I wanted a bunch of them. But when I got saved, my eyes and ears got 'transplants.' Suddenly I could see what the old saying 'Beauty is only skin deep' really means. A woman, like a movie star, may look gorgeous at a distance, especially when you don't know her at all. But once you meet her, that beauty starts to require a whole lot more. It requires 'the hidden person of the heart' (1 Pet. 3:4).

"Christ lights up a woman. When she's really given her life to Christ, you know you're not with just another body. When she smiles at you and shows you any attention at all, you feel great. You're with somebody you admire and can easily respect. Thank God for every single Christian female."

The Importance of Friends

Whether or not you ever date, following the advice in this chapter should increase your circle of friends.

In his book *Bonding* (Word), Donald Joy says that everyone needs about thirty meaningful relationships to maintain emotional health. As that number dwindles, a person becomes unhealthily dependent on a few individuals.

As you make new acquaintances, you will have to make choices about meaningful friendships. The Living Bible says, "A mirror reflects a man's face, but what he is really like is shown by the kind of friends he chooses" (Prov. 27:19).

I have marveled at the amazing ability of teenagers who are hostile toward their parents to find others with the same attitude within twenty-four hours of arrival at a teen camp. People choose the kind of friends that suit their needs.

I don't mean to imply that people will come flocking to you. Positive people who love the Lord are both attractive and shunned, depending on whom they are around. Their quick ability to care and forgive, their faith in the midst of a crumbling world, their desire to do the right thing even when wrong would be easier — these qualities often repulse those who love sin. During His earthly lifetime Jesus was rejected not only by the world but by His grumbling brothers (John 7:2-5). Live for Christ no matter what relationship it costs you.

First Corinthians 15:33 warns against keeping company with those whose morals are weak or corrupt. Christians may wrongly assume they should keep close to old friends who are immoral so they can be a witness to those friends. But if "bad company corrupts good morals," then the Christian *will* be corrupted by the immoral, not vice versa.

That doesn't mean you should be rude to or shun the immoral. But to keep an honest witness and to keep your own morals pure, you need to distance yourself. Be available for conversation when they want to get real answers for life. Show them your Christlike love always. Like them. But don't *be* like them. Christ's enemies are not good friends.

What if a "good" friend goes "bad"? Suppose, for example, a friend of yours joined the New Age movement or some other part of the occult. Suppose a friend got into drugs or alcohol or began to mock God and all that Christians stand for. You would, of course, first try to "restore such a one in a spirit of gentleness" (Gal. 6:1). But if this person refused to be restored spiritually, you would have to do perhaps the hardest thing you will ever do — separate yourself from that friend. God tells you, "Come out from their midst and be separate" (2 Cor. 6:17). The whole point of 2 Corinthians 6:14-7:1 is to express the need to "turn away from everything wrong, whether of body or spirit, and purify ourselves, living in the wholesome fear of God, giving ourselves to Him alone" (7:1, LB).

Note that the prodigal son's father led him back to Christ by leaving the porch light on (Luke 15:11-24). Had he rushed out to the pigpen and sobbed because his son wouldn't come home, he might well have turned his son off. Had he rented a truck with giant loudspeakers on top and driven by the pigpen screaming, "Repent, you dirty sinner!" there most likely would have been nothing but anger and embarrassment from the son toward his dad. Instead, the father must have prayed and waited for his son to come to his senses. No one can explain the perfect timing of the Lord. It is a mystery beyond human comprehension. But God's timing *is* perfect, and when we refuse to worry about people but instead pray for them, God can wake the sinner up.

Who are your closest friends? What input for good or bad are they having on your thought life? Is it time you became more distant from any of them? Have you noticed people who are a positive witness for Christ and make you glad to be around them? Is it possible God has shown these people to you so that you will draw closer to them?

On the other hand, if you were another person, would you like to be a friend of yours? If not, it's time to change your ways.

Be a Friend

A man who has friends must himself be friendly (Prov. 18:24, NKJV).

What is a friend? Friends are those rare people who ask how we are and then wait to hear the answer. Friends knock before they enter, not after they leave. A friend is a person who can step on your toes without messing up your shine.[3] Friends care. They can laugh with you and cry with you and not be embarrassed to do either one (Rom. 12:15). Friends are honestly interested in everything about you, and you could trust them with the most private information in the world. Friends want you to be closer to Christ than to them. Friends are those who speak to you when others won't. A friend is one who knows all your faults but likes you anyway. Real friends aren't friends because of your looks — or their looks — but because of your heart.

Study the above paragraph. Don't ask yourself how many friends you have. Ask yourself how many people you are befriending.

The best vitamin
for making friends is B1.

Questions for Reflection and Discussion

1. Write an answer to the professor's letter preceding chapter 5. Especially add any further thoughts of your own about dating not covered in chapter 5.

2. Reflect on the discussion of friendship in this chapter. How would you define friendship? Think of some of the friends you have now. What are some of the characteristics you admire most about them? What characteristics do you think they admire most in you? Have you had to work to make these friendships successful? How would the idea of pursuing friendship change the way you think about dating? Write down your answers. Keep the list of what people admire about you. Discuss the other questions.

3. Read the story of David and Jonathan as recorded in the books of 1 and 2 Samuel, beginning directly after David slew Goliath (1 Sam. 18). Write down everything you can learn about friendship from this story. What do these verses say about friendships and the need to choose your friends carefully?

4. First Timothy 4:12 is an important verse for all singles to understand. Carefully read this verse using several different translations. After doing so, write out your own definitions to each point. Can you think of some practical ways to grow in each area? Discuss each point.

5. Read 2 Corinthians 6:14-7:1. In light of this passage, consider verse 17 carefully. Suppose a close friend of yours joined the New Age movement or some other cult or did some other thing covered in this passage. How would you react? What could you do to help them break free? What if they wouldn't listen to you? What would be the proper steps to take to "come out from their midst and be separate"? Write down your answers and then discuss this thoroughly.

Dear Ray,

I'm pregnant and not married. I never thought it would happen to me. I got through college without sex. I resisted every temptation. Now, because I dated one unsaved guy, I am going to have his baby. Before we knew about the baby, he told me he loved me. That's a joke. He's gone. Not that I would have married him anyway. But someday my baby will want to know where his or her dad is. I'm already tongue-tied trying to think of how I'll answer.

Here are some questions for you: (1) My folks liked him a lot. They encouraged me to date him. They're Christians too. How do I forgive them? (2) Should I have ever dated him? In fact, should I have ever dated any guy? The Christians all tried to paw me. What good is dating? (3) I still want to get married to a great Christian guy sometime, if I can ever find one. Do I have a right to pray for that to happen anymore? Will God even hear my prayers anymore? (4) I won't marry this unsaved jerk. But suppose he comes back into my life and wants to live with me. Should I let him — to give my baby his or her rightful dad?

I'm looking forward to attending your Singles Plus seminar in about a month. I wish I'd attended it before I ever met this guy.

Growing Bigger Every Day

*Though one may be
overpowered by another,
two can withstand him.
And a threefold cord
is not quickly broken.*
            Ecclesiastes 4:12, NKJV

SIX

ESSENTIAL POTENTIAL

Marriage is like picking what you'll
cat out of a box of toadstools and mushrooms.
You might like what you find,
but you'd better choose carefully.
Your whole life is at stake!

Step One: Valentine's Day Every Day

Some enchanted evening you will see a stranger across a crowded room. Suddenly your heart will sound like a Salvation Army drum. You have found him (or her) at last. Perfect. Not one flaw. You were made for each other. Being together is heaven. When you are separated, time stands still. You talk on the phone for hours, whether you have anything to say or not. You agree with everything this person says, even if you don't agree. You write his or her name on every piece of paper you can find. You talk about the person constantly. He or she is the last thought at night and the first thought each morning. You're sure you are in love — but this is a dream state, not reality.

Step Two: Going Steady

Your infatuation now has a ring to it. Or a pin. Or you exchange key chains, or teeth. Whether or not you declare it officially, you are now paired together exclusively. You may be telling each other you love each other. You may also be talking about "If we ever get married...." However, there is a nagging thought in your mind that you really don't know enough about this person to be sure you would be happy for a lifetime of marriage. You keep trying to push that thought away. You are meeting his or her closest friends and parents. You aren't sure whether they like you. You wonder what they say about you in private. You may begin regretting that you gave away your tooth.

Step Three: Double Jeopardy

One of you recognizes something unlikable about the other. It may be a small thing: a zit; he laughs too loud; she is silent when you want to talk; he eats onions and breathes on you. You are amazed to discover she isn't perfect. You struggle to keep your happiness kite in the air, but reality is forcing it down. You decide you'll tell him or her what's wrong and see if things change. You believe if he or she really loves you, he or she *will* change. But you talk, and he or she just gets defensive, then gives you a list of your faults. Suddenly both of you are privately wondering whether you haven't been seeing too much of each other. You may wonder that out loud. You have an argument that may end in tears. You may ask for your key chain back. Most romantic relationships terminate at this point.

Step Four: Friends

After withdrawing from each other, you both miss each other very much. You get to thinking about that zit and tell yourself it was really kind of cute. You get together by telephone, and both of you say, "I'm sorry." You make a date. You decide to be just good friends. You still think about marriage with this person, but you now notice his or her real flaws. You also think much more realistically about his or her walk with Christ, temperament, goals, interests, hobbies, feelings about children and so forth. You make a crucial decision at this point about each of these areas and much more. You contemplate how this person would fit into a lifetime with you. You realize you don't love this person yet. You decide at this point whether you would ever want to marry this person. If the answer is no, you may stop dating.

If this person is one you still may want to marry, and he or she feels the same way about you, you date awhile and then become engaged. But, even then, please remember that, except for receiving Jesus Christ as your Lord, *marriage* is the biggest decision you will ever make.

Is Going Steady Appropriate?

Engagement is appropriate for adults who plan to marry. Before that, I'm not sure an exclusive relationship is appropriate. Since the Bible is silent about the subject, I can only give my views gleaned from what I've observed after hearing reports from at least a thousand people who did go steady at some point in their lives (including me). They consistently point out these problems:

1. *Going steady cuts off all other opportunities to date*. Many times each year I hear the tale of a wife, or sometimes a husband, who wants out of a marriage: "I didn't have a chance to live. He (or she) was the only person I ever dated. We went steady right from the start. I found out too late that I wanted another kind of person." What seemed romantic or secure in the dating stage now appears to be a ball and chain.

2. *Familiarity breeds contempt*. When a couple is constantly together too long before marriage (more than two years), familiarity tends to breed contempt. Later in this book I'll talk about the law of diminishing returns in regard to the physical relationship.

It is not unusual to hear a girl say, "My boyfriend takes me for granted. When we first started dating, he would phone and ask me if I wanted to go to such-and-such a place. He took me out. We had lots of fun. Now he drops by my house unannounced to spend the evening. Instead of going someplace, he just wants to watch television or make out."

3. *Going steady happens too long before marriage*. Two sixteen-year-olds going steady almost always face the extreme temptations of having sex before marriage or marrying too young. Statistics show that anyone dating before the age of sixteen runs the greatest risk of conceiving a child or impregnating a woman out of wedlock. Dating before age sixteen is simply too young because of the long span of time that should occur before marriage.

Getting to Know You

You don't need to be going steady to get to know someone, and there's no substitute for knowing whom you're considering as a marriage partner.

Dating is a mini-picture of what marriage with your date might be like. Granted, it is a fuzzy picture, because so much changes when a couple actually marries. That means things will get worse. Every serious study of the first year of marriage shows that males tend to be far less romantic after marriage than before it. Women tend to miss the romance of dating almost immediately after their honeymoon. A great deal of this has to do with the fact that men are conquer-oriented. Forty-nine percent of couples in the first year of their marriage report they are having big problems with each other. This is often because the guy feels he's "bagged his dear." So he turns to other worlds to conquer.

If either the male or female is being treated poorly by a date, he or she can expect a thousand times worse treatment should the two ever marry.

Dating gives the dater an up-close look at the person dated. Each date with any one person adds to the picture. When marriage is even a possibility, the dater had better look very hard!

Two primary reasons so many divorces take place in America today are (1) the persons who married didn't know each other well enough to be reasonably certain the other would be a great marriage partner for a lifetime; (2) the persons who married didn't know themselves well enough to be reasonably certain they would be great marriage partners for a lifetime.

A lifetime is a very long time. If you are thirty-five or younger and marry within the next two or three years (and if you and your spouse are committed to keeping Jesus Christ at the center of your marriage), you will probably end up married longer than you have been single. With that in mind, you had better be very, very careful about whom you choose for your lifetime.

Let's examine some traits you should look for in someone you're considering as a spouse.

Potentially Outstanding Marriage Partners
Have Jesus Christ as Lord of Their Lives

God can make a bad marriage good, but how much better to start with a great marriage that gets better all the time. Remember: "Unless the Lord builds the house, they labor in vain who build it" (Ps. 127:1). The only way to ensure a great marriage is to start out the marriage with Him in the center of it.

Jesus Christ must be the third partner in a marriage if the love-cord is to be strong (Eccl. 4:12).

One of the greatest lies the devil tells single Christians is, "Marry this unsaved person, and then you can lead him or her to Christ." But years later wives and husbands tell me, "My spouse says, 'Why should I change? You love me as I am, or you wouldn't have married me!' "

New Christians (for two years or less), even though they are growing in Christ, are not yet good marriage material. They need to be watched, as one would watch a young child, to see that they are maturing into healthy Christians. If you or your true love is a new Christian, slow down your relationship; wait for Christian maturity before you marry.

Contrary to most Bible translations in English, the original text of Proverbs 18:22 does not say, "He who finds a wife finds a good thing." The Amplified Bible is closer to God's statement: "He who finds a [true] wife finds a good thing, and obtains favor of the Lord." It is a good, faithful Christian wife who brings the blessings of the Lord — not just any wife. The same is true about marrying a good, faithful Christian husband. Accept no substitutes.

Potentially Outstanding Marriage Partners
Worship Together

Some denominational differences involve minor issues in church government or theology. But some denominational differences are major, and conflicting loyalties can cause major problems in a marriage.

One example: What if one marriage partner believes speaking in tongues is a vital component of prayer and worship, while the other believes speaking in tongues died out after the first century? The Bible can easily settle such controversy if Christians will turn to it without bias, but the devil has always used preconceived prejudice to divide God's people. Which church will this couple attend? A charismatic or Pentecostal church where one of the partners wants to rebuke anyone who speaks in tongues? Or a church that the charismatic partner sees as dry and lacking the Spirit's power?

In either case, one (often both) will usually remain unhappy. The one who considers him or herself sacrificial will often say, "I'm not getting anything out of the church service."

Division over Christ's church often causes great division in marriage. Catholic-Protestant debates or high church-low church conflicts have sent many couples to the divorce court, especially when the question arises, "Where will our child attend?" All such matters need to be decided honestly and fully before a couple ever marries. Couples who love Jesus Christ and each other and are willing to die to man-made traditions and prejudices can find God's will and agree about the church they should attend. A loving, Christ-centered counselor can often be a great help as all such matters are being discussed. If there is still disagreement about these things before marriage, the marriage should not take place.

But if any of you lacks wisdom, let him [or her] ask of God, who gives

105

to all...generously and without reproach, and it will be given.... But let him [or her] ask in faith without any doubting, for the one who doubts is like the surf of the sea driven and tossed by the wind (James 1:5-6).

God's will always agrees with God's Word.

Potentially Outstanding Marriage Partners
Are Able to Stay on Top of Their Problems

Don't plan a wedding if you or your love is in turmoil.

If you are considering marriage, how quick is your prospective spouse to pray about problems and believe God will work everything out? How positive is he or she about life? Living the rest of your life with someone who constantly goes into tailspins isn't going to make you or your children very happy. Is every phone conversation a soap opera of sad commentary? Is that what you want for the rest of your life?

Luke 1:37 tells us, "For nothing will be impossible with God." You don't have a problem He can't work out — if you turn that problem over to Him. It doesn't matter how painful your situation is, God cares. Tell Him about it (1 Pet. 5:6-7). Ask Him what to do (James 1:5-8). Be sure what you think you heard Him say agrees with His written Word (John 8:31-32). Obey Him (John 7:17; Rom. 12:2). Trust Him (Is. 26:3-4).

God won't always do *your* will. But when He doesn't, it is because He will do "beyond all that [you] ask or think" (Eph. 3:20).

If you're the Florence Nightingale type, become a nurse. But don't tie yourself to unhappiness on purpose. Be sure your prospective mate has the inner security from Jesus Christ that will add to the strength you have from Him. Accept no substitutes.

Potentially Outstanding Marriage Partners
Are Adaptable and Flexible

Life itself is a continuous process of getting used to the unexpected — sometimes wonderful, sometimes tragic.

If you're employed, do you think you'll be at your present job all your life? You may. You may not. Changes will come whether you trust in the Lord or not (Ps. 37:3-6). But if you're not flexible and adaptable as you trust in Him, those changes may very well frighten you.

How do you — and your date — react when the other calls at the last minute to change plans? "I have to work late," or "The car won't start." Is the answer,

"Oh, that's OK. I'm so glad you called"? Or does someone fall apart, attacking the other for not keeping his or her word?

First Corinthians 13:4 says, "Love is patient, love is kind." Marry someone who blows up at the drop of a hat, shouts when angry and is often irritated, and you'll stay nervous and jumpy, just waiting for the next explosion. You likely will also regret your decision for the rest of your life.

The patient, flexible person can wait without anxiety. A patient person doesn't keep staring at a clock telling you to hurry up. If you have to go somewhere for a day or a year, a patient, flexible person will wait for you — if he or she really loves you.

How you and your date face crises with each other will give you another answer as to whether or not you should marry.

Potentially Outstanding Marriage Partners Exhibit Self-Control

We live in a very angry nation.

Domestic violence is the number-one cause of all physical injury to women in the United States. Every fifteen seconds a woman is beaten. According to the FBI, 40 percent of all murdered women are killed by their partners. Two out of three pregnant women treated in emergency rooms have been beaten. Four to six million women will be beaten this year. Sixty-five percent of all young men incarcerated for murder are there for having killed their mother's battering husband or friend.

According to one report, 250,000 men yearly are battered so severely by women that they require medical attention. Another report says up to one million men a year are battered by women. Fifty percent of women and 20 percent of men say they've been slapped very hard by their lover within the past year. Fear and the risk of embarrassment keep domestic violence probably the single most unreported crime in America.

Then there's the issue of child abuse, which *kills* two to five children every day in America. Isaiah 58:4 warns of those who "strike with a wicked fist." Anger kills.

If you know the one you are dating has a bad temper, you are foolish to continue your relationship. Why risk the lives and health of you and your children?

When Jesus said, "Do good to those who hate you" (Luke 6:27), He was saying we are to choose to do God's highest good for those who perform hateful acts toward us. God's highest good is never to allow them to continue the acts, but to stop them from further harming themselves or others. Pastors, counselors and well-meaning friends who try to put Band-Aids on bullet holes with advice like "Just hang in there. Keep loving and praying for the abuser" may feel spiritual, but they are giving ungodly counsel. They may, in fact, be leading to the murder of one or more persons.

How can you know if you really need help with an abuser? Marilyn Post of the Domestic Violence Project Learning Center in Quincy, Illinois, offers the following questions you need to answer. If the answers describe the person in question, call Marilyn for further help at (217) 222-3711.

1. Do they have problems with most authority figures — that is, parents, pastors, bosses, the police?

2. Must they always win and never lose? Do they want to get revenge if they lose?

3. Do they drive with rage? Are they offensive drivers who feel others' mistakes while driving are directed toward them?

4. Are they cruel to animals?

5. Are they uncomfortable with their own feelings and/or contemptuous of others' weaknesses?

6. Do they seem to have different personalities for different occasions? Do their personalities change to fit whatever people or group of people they are with?

7. Do they have a distorted view of reality? Do they rationalize away their sin with statements that begin "I have a right to...," and then try to tell you why or give no reason?

8. Do they have an arrogant, flamboyant, big-shot way of behaving that always tries to impress people?

9. Do they put conditions on their love — "If you loved me, you'd..." — and then threaten to withdraw if you won't cooperate?

10. Do they track all of your time and demand to know where you have been when you are away from them even for a few hours?

11. Do they discourage you from keeping a warm relationship with your family and friends?

12. Do they criticize you for little things that don't matter?

13. Do they take drugs or drink alcohol? If so, do they get angry while doing it?

14. Do they constantly accuse you of being unfaithful to them?

15. Do they ever threaten to hurt you or your children?

16. Do they hit, slap, punch, kick or bite you or your children?

17. Have they ever used or threatened to use a weapon against you?

18. Do they prevent you from leaving your house or theirs for any reason?

19. Do they try to control your finances and complain if you spend any money?

20. Do they humiliate you in front of others or tear you apart verbally when you are alone?

21. Do they destroy your personal property?

There's an apple tree in our yard. It produces wonderful, healthy apples every apple season — because it's a wonderfully healthy apple tree. I have never heard it groan and strain to produce an apple. The apples grow because the tree is whole. How whole are you? How whole is your intended? Do some very careful "fruit inspection" of Galatians 5:22-23, which lists the fruit of the Spirit — including *self-control*. Jesus makes all the difference.

Potentially Outstanding Marriage Partners
Don't Drink Alcohol, Smoke Anything or Do Drugs

Casual drinking and casual drugs are like casual dying. It can't be done. I care deeply about singles, and I know the life choices they make will make them either very happy or very sorry. So please understand my heart as I write this next sentence: Never date or marry a person who drinks alcohol for the fun of it, smokes anything but ham or salmon, or uses drugs for the sake of getting a thrill. A comparison of various divorce statistics shows that drug or alcohol abuse is the sixth-ranked cause of divorce in the United States.

I don't believe drinking an occasional beer or glass of wine is necessarily a sin. It depends a great deal on the motives of the person and whether he or she stops before his or her tolerance level becomes intolerant.

There are Christian homes where champagne or another form of alcohol is used for special toasts during celebrations. Several denominations serve wine for their communion services. If such drinking is done in careful moderation where not one person becomes addicted or gets intoxicated, and if participants honestly feel no conviction about it in their own spirits, then who am I to tell them they may be stumbling blocks for weaker people? But I do advise everyone to study Romans 14:13-15 and 20-23 in this light.

The problem of drinking is very complex. Today ten million American adults and five million teenagers and adolescents are alcoholics. More than half of all automobile fatalities occur because of alcohol. Hardly anyone, Christian or not, can determine his or her alcohol tolerance level unless that person has been drunk several times, and by then the tolerance level may not mean anything.

The heartbreaking stories I hear at Marriage Plus seminars would make you understand why I urge you not to date anyone who thinks he or she deserves an occasional drink. That's the way it starts out, but too many husbands or wives surrender to the bottle. The results? Children humiliated, beaten, sexually abused; spousal violence; codependents growing up and marrying alcoholics because they know only one relational style — trying to rescue and change what will not change. I don't hear a few of these stories; I hear a perpetual stream of them.

But equally heartbreaking stories come out at the Singles Plus seminars: date rape, violence, severe emotional trauma, unwanted pregnancy, automobile accidents. It took only one drink in some cases to begin a completely destructive personality change, or to cause injury or death in an accident. Alcohol doesn't have the remotest connection with "life more abundantly" (John 10:10).

Smoking, like alcohol or drugs, has been called suicide on the installment plan. Smoking is the leading cause of premature death in the United States. In spite of fewer people smoking today — 29 percent now versus 40 percent in 1965 — smoking-related deaths are expected to continue to rise in America for several years.

Recent reports indicate that sidestream smoke — living with a smoker — can even kill the nonsmoker more quickly than the one who smokes. As a parent, you'd do everything you could to protect your child's health. Well, protect it — and your own — by not smoking and not dating a smoker.

Finally, the National Highway Traffic Safety Administration says 10 to 22 percent (depending on the state) of all drivers in serious car crashes have drugs other than alcohol in their systems. And I don't even have room here to cover the serious physical and psychological damage drugs cause to the user and the unborn children of drug-using mothers.

The Bible condemns drug abuse. Two Greek words, translated in most Bibles as "sorcerers," are actually *pharmakeion* and *pharmakeia*, from which we get our word *pharmacy*. But these words aren't referring to a typical pharmacist.

Pharmakeion, "one who uses drugs for the purpose of enchantment," is found in Galatians 5:20. "Now the deeds of the flesh are evident, which are: immorality, impurity, sensuality, idolatry, *sorcery*...and things like these, of which I forewarn you just as I have forewarned you that those who practice such things shall not inherit the kingdom of God" (vv. 19-21, italics mine). According to Revelation 9:21 (where "pharmakeia" is again used), the use of any drug for enchantment (getting a "high," turning on, dropping out) leads to hell now and eternally, unless it is repented of and stopped.

The other Greek word, *pharmakeia*, translated into English as "sorcerers" in Revelation 21:8 and Revelation 22:15, actually means "one who provides drugs for the purpose of enchantment." In both verses, all *pharmakeia* are in hell eternally. Therefore, selling or giving away drugs so that others can get an emotional kick will send the unrepentant provider to hell.

No one but you can ultimately make you stop drugs or avoid them or people who use them. Jesus Christ will give you the total power to stop, if you'll surrender to Him. If you marry someone who feels it is necessary to indulge in drugs, you will pay a terrible price. It could be mourning their death. It could be your own death or your child's. It could be years of heartache. It's often all three. It's up to you.

Potentially Outstanding Marriage Partners
Agree on How to Raise Children

First, a person who does not like children or young people almost always carries emotional wounds that have not been healed. That person is a poor choice for marriage. Instead, they need Christ-centered counseling.

Think about your childhood and teen years. How has the way you were raised affected you? What role did your parents play in shaping the way you think today? What kind of a parent would you be? What kind of an adult are you going to raise? Children *are* the future.

A minister once asked a group of Sunday school children, "Why do you love God?" One little boy answered, "Well, I don't know, sir. I guess it just runs in the family." Will loving God "run in the family" if you marry the person you're dating?

When you marry, you'll be picking out your kids' father or mother. Would your present choice meet their needs?

What are your attitudes toward discipline, including spankings; curfew; church attendance? Which church? What movies should children or teenagers be allowed to see, if any? How much money should they be allowed to have? When should teenagers be allowed to date?

Before marriage, two *must* agree regarding the raising of children. If you aren't agreed, you are headed for a serious showdown when the baby arrives. The showdown and shoot-out between Mom and Dad have left millions of children out in the cold. Disagreement over how to raise children is one of the major reasons for divorce.

To help you think through this crucial area together, you may want to order my two cassette tapes titled "Raising Children."

Potentially Outstanding Marriage Partners
Know How to Give and Receive Love

Some people seem capable of giving love but not receiving love. Others seem able to receive but not give it. An outstanding marriage partner can do both.

Giving yourself isn't enough to prove love. "And if I give all my possessions to feed the poor, and if I deliver my body to be burned, but do not have love, it profits me nothing" (1 Cor. 13:3). Motives matter. Are your actions because of your love of God and others?

111

Do you like to give? Does it delight you to delight others? The guy who brings flowers to his date because he knows she loves them may well be bringing God's love with those flowers. It isn't wrong at all that he feels good when she thanks him for the flowers. He's made her happy. That's God's plan. Everything changes, however, if he has an ulterior motive in his action.

What are your motives in giving to anyone? What is your motive for giving to your date? Whether they think it or not, guys who say, "I paid for her dinner and movie, and now I deserve a kiss, at least" are believing they've dated a prostitute. After all, men *buy* their "rights" to a prostitute.

"Love does not demand its own way" (1 Cor. 13:5, LB). If you or the one you are dating is not a Christian giver, one of you will live with a self-centered, ego-feeding person. If that person is you, your selfishness will eventually destroy you unless you repent. If the selfish person is the one you're dating, discontinue the relationship. No matter how much it hurts now, you risk throwing away your close walk with Christ; because of that person's selfishness, they will always be jealous of Him.

When Jesus said, "By this all men will know that you are My disciples, if you have love for one another" (John 13:35), He was including both the ability to give it and to receive it. Anyone who can't do both is best eliminated from your datebook.

Potentially Outstanding Marriage Partners
Have Their Finances in Order

Approximately one in two American marriages ends in divorce, and one in two American couples marries without any financial security. I can't help but believe there's a correlation between the statistics.

It is not fair to enter a marriage without a clear understanding of how to stay financially secure and a commitment to staying that way. Maturity means being able to stand on your own two feet as you follow Jesus Christ. The kind of maturity marriage requires means being able to stand on your own four feet as you follow Jesus Christ.

How are you doing with your finances? Are you tithing? Are you giving God offerings above your tithes? Are you buying most things with cash? Are you paying your bills on time? Are you saving money for the future? Have you invested some of your money so that your investment is appreciating?

If the answer to any of these questions is no, let me recommend the writings of Larry Burkett, Ron Blue and Malcolm MacGregor, which offer clear, biblical teaching on personal finance. My two cassettes "God's Plan for Abundant Finance" are available from my office.

A word to men: First Timothy 5:8 says the husband is responsible for being the provider in a marriage. So if you are male and are not (1) tithing, (2) cheerfully giving offerings to God above your tithe (2 Cor. 9:6-8) and (3) financially healthy, please, I beg you, don't get married. All you'll do is end up keeping the one you say you love dirt poor and wishing she'd never married you.

A word to women: If you are always spending and always broke, change your ways before you change your name. Unless you are marrying a millionaire, you'll end up keeping him dirt poor and both of you unhappy. Reading and listening to the above resources — and following the teachings — will "make you free" (John 8:31-32).

Potentially Outstanding Marriage Partners
Trust Each Other

Jealous people keep you from making any real friends, because they demand exclusive rights to you. They live in constant fear that they will lose you to someone else. They will want to go steady or get engaged *fast* to cut off all competition. They will rob you of your freedom to make choices on your own. To marry a jealous person is to stay lonely all your life.

People who aren't jealous trust you. They believe God can lead you as well as them. They are glad you have many good friends, because it confirms how likable you are. They can let you make up your mind without rushing you for decisions. They want, most of all, for you to stay close to Christ and to follow Him wherever He leads you. You know they care about you whether you are with them or not. Dating them is great, because they are not worried about anyone else you might also like.

Never marry anyone you don't completely trust, and trust is like a bank: You build it up through daily deposits. So any date caught in a lie is poor marriage material. If you don't trust someone now, you will trust him or her far less if you marry him or her — and you'll have a miserable, unhappy marriage. Instead, wake up or break up now.

Potentially Outstanding Marriage Partners
Have an Understanding Spirit

Romans 12:15 instructs us to "rejoice with those who rejoice, and weep with those who weep." I like rejoicing. Weeping is far more painful. But God says both are required if we are to love.

Webster's New World Dictionary defines *empathy* as "the projection of one's own personality into the personality of another in order to understand him better;

the ability to share in another's emotions or feelings." Empathy is an absolute necessity in marriage. Without it you carry the constant pain of knowing that the person who is supposed to care about you most doesn't even try.

How well do you empathize with others? Do you really care, deep down inside, when someone else is hurting? Does someone's pain have to make sense to you before you care, or is the pain alone enough to make you care?

On the other hand, how much do you — or your date — "rejoice with those who rejoice"? If one of you loses a game to the other, do you rejoice for the winner and stay thankful that you both had fun together? Or does the loser call the winner lucky and make excuses for the loss? Are you a good sport?

Sadly, dates try harder to empathize than spouses do. If one of you lacks empathy, marriage will most likely mean rejoicing and weeping by yourself.

Potentially Outstanding Marriage Partners
Share Interests

"Can two walk together, unless they are agreed?" (Amos 3:3, NKJV). The answer seems obvious. Who wants to walk with someone with whom you don't agree? Incompatible leisure-time activities are the seventh-ranked cause of divorce.

The best marriages join two people with similar interests. They like to go to the same places, worship in the same church, work on the same kinds of projects, laugh at the same jokes, eat the same kinds of food, spend leisure time together. The list can go on and on. Yet you don't have to be Siamese twins. A puzzle isn't exciting because the pieces are all alike, but because the pieces complete each other

I'm often asked, When does friendship end and love begin in a male-female relationship? The truth is, friendship never stops if real love is present in the relationship. In any good marriage a husband and wife must *love* and *like* each other. The person you marry should also be your best friend.

Ask your boyfriend or girlfriend to write down a list of things he or she really enjoys doing. Suggest that the list be as long as possible. Don't explain why you're making the request.

Make the same kind of list for yourself. Then compare the two lists. Working together, answer two big questions: Do you share a lot of similar interests? Will you gladly (not with gritted teeth) accept each other's differences? If the answer to both questions is yes, you'll probably enjoy life and leisure together.

While I'm talking about interests, let me mention friends. Some like loud people; others enjoy only the quiet type. Some like to laugh a lot; others choose very solemn peers. Choice of friends also involves morals, habits, behavior and so forth. Do you like your boyfriend's or girlfriend's other best friends? Does he or she like your friends? Remember, "A mirror reflects a man's face, but what he is really like is shown by the kind of friends he chooses" (Prov. 27:19, LB). Remember, even if you move somewhere else, your spouse will almost always choose friends just like the ones he or she has chosen now.

Friends can help make marriage joyful or tear it apart. The tug-of-war that goes on between friends, wives and husbands pulls multitudes of marriages into divorce court every year.

Potentially Outstanding Marriage Partners
Have Similar Habits

Even with many common interests, two people can have vastly different habit patterns. One will be a morning person and one a night owl. One will squeeze the toothpaste from the center of the tube, and the other only from the bottom of the tube. One will like the temperature hot; the other wants to freeze to death. Some of these things will be learned as you're dating. But others will usually be discovered after marriage.

In dating, opposites attract. Beyond appearance, the first real attraction you feel toward someone usually is an ingredient missing in yourself. You admire someone who says or does things the way you don't. But after marriage these same opposites seem to rear their ugly heads. Someone has rightly said, "Love is blind, and marriage is an eye-opener!"

If you find yourselves terribly incompatible now, please don't lie to each other and lead each other on. Love demands maturity. There's one great thing about dating that won't remain true after marriage. Before you walk the aisle, flaws can be more easily corrected. If either of you sees a flaw that you know will cause major problems, either stop the habit or leave the relationship. If the flaw doesn't go, the possibility of marriage should. Why enter marriage knowing that something is going to make living together an unhappy experience for the rest of your lives?

Potentially Outstanding Marriage Partners
Have Good Communication Skills

Marriage makes communication crucial. In studying and comparing divorce-statistic lists, I have found that communication breakdown is almost always the number-one reason for divorce. Every problem that arises requires communication that doesn't stop with "I'd rather not talk about it." Unless you're talking intently on your dates about a lot more than cars, movies, pizza or the million-dollar home you'll someday enjoy together, you won't be ready for communication in marriage.

The average American couple communicates with each other twelve minutes a week. ("Pass the cornflakes" is not considered communication.) The tragedy of that fact and the subsequent divorces speak for themselves.

One aspect of communication is humility. Any person who isn't humble enough to say "I'm sorry" when he or she has made a mistake should be considered unmarriageable. In marriage, the words "I'm sorry" become two of the most important for bringing healing to a strained relationship. Few learn to say these words after they're married if they haven't learned to say them before marriage.

Norm Wright has written several excellent books (published by Gospel Light and Harvest House) on this subject. For further help, you might want to send for my cassette tapes titled "How to Communicate."

Three More Qualities

Let me give you three more qualities you should consider when looking for a marriage partner. These qualities repeatedly show up in statistical reports of marriages that last or don't last. Though they may not be as essential as ones given earlier in the chapter, these three characteristics should be evaluated as part of any marriage discussion.

Potentially outstanding marriage partners have similar parental backgrounds. Take one adult who has grown up with a silver spoon in his or her mouth and another who has grown up on the wrong side of the tracks, and you'll nearly always find they think very different kinds of thoughts.

For example, the one raised with ready money may have learned the habit of buying things, of spending money. The one raised in poverty may have pinched pennies. Imagine the problems *that* can cause once these two marry.

Two people with similar parental backgrounds usually have one less problem to face in becoming one. Because they've been trained up in parallel environments, they relate to the whole world from a unified perspective. There will always be differences between any two humans, but peas from the same pod tend to agree more quickly.

Potentially outstanding marriage partners are similar in age. The Bible does not seem to present age differences as a barrier to marriage.

As a rule of thumb, however, marriages that last generally have husbands no more than seven years older than their wives and wives no more than three years older than their husbands.

Two problems are usually related to husbands much older than their wives. First, men tend to die younger than women, leaving them widows. Most American married women are eventually widowed. Second, husbands much older than their wives tend to run out of energy long before younger, vibrant women do. Overnight the wife's dashing husband may seem like her grandpa. If she goes out often, leaving him at home, the two can end up living very separate, unhappy lives.

Aging is the problem most often associated with an older woman marrying a much younger man. A forty-year-old woman and a twenty-five-year-old man may both look like Hollywood glamour types. But when she turns sixty, and he is a young forty-five, she may fear losing him to someone else, even if he has no such intentions. The nagging fears that he may be unfaithful may eventually cause arguments and accusations that drive a deep wedge between the two.

Faithfulness to Christ means faithfulness to a spouse. But it is wise to give careful consideration to potential future heartaches when considering marriage to a man or woman much older or younger than yourself.

Potentially outstanding marriage partners have similar race and cultural backgrounds. Like it or not, one's childhood makes a great difference in one's adulthood. Individual family bias, quite aside from cultural or regional bias, can plant seeds of hatred in a young heart toward any group that appears different from "our kind." The verse "Train up a child in the way he should go, even when he is old he will not depart from it" (Prov. 22:6) doesn't refer only to godly families. It is very hard to re-educate early cultural training in *any* human. The apostle Paul said that even "godly" Peter forgot what he said in Acts 10:34-35; Paul had to remind him of it when Peter (also called Cephas) later again favored the Jews over the Gentiles (Gal. 2:11-16). Paul communicated God's heart about all mankind, no matter what race or nationality: "There is no distinction" (Rom. 3:22).

At the Church on the Way in Van Nuys, California, our elder-body includes several interracial couples who are among the finest couples I have ever met. Their marriages are an example to us all. When two single Christians of differing skin pigmentation fall in love and want to marry (and qualify in every other way), no one should interfere. The marriage of Moses to a Cushite woman was interracial, and God defended him (Numbers 12).

However, some painful divorces are caused because the couple couldn't stand the cruelty of those who opposed them. Before an interracial marriage occurs, both the man and woman need to answer some serious questions forthrightly.

1. If people are cruel in their words or actions to either of you because of your marriage, will both of you be able to maintain your Christian testimony and your love for each other? Are you committed to a lifelong marriage in spite of tribulations (John 16:33)?

2. In spite of cruelty, will you be able to grow in your love for Jesus Christ and "love your enemies, and pray for those who persecute you" (Matt. 5:44)?

3. How will you react to prejudice that harms your child or children, mentally

or physically? Will you be able to maintain your walk with Jesus Christ and each other? Will you still be able to forgive those who sin against you (Matt. 6:12, 14-15)?

How unfortunate that any two Christians who plan to marry should have to consider such questions. But with hatred of all kinds being spewed out toward the human race, it would be wise for any two Christians contemplating marriage to answer the above questions.

You may be saying, But I can't find anyone who is single and meets all of these requirements. Maybe you haven't met him or her yet, but I have met many singles who fit all these potentialities. They are worth waiting for!

There may not be "one special someone" for you somewhere. You could marry any one of hundreds of people who — if you both followed God's directions — would be a great partner for you. But God wants the best for your whole life. So you've got to be wise in choosing. Unless you travel through the terrible sorrow of divorce or widowhood, you only get to choose once. Please keep this book handy as a manual for careful and prayerful selection of that most difficult of life's choices — the right mate.

Troubles are like a baby's diapers.
They've got to be changed
when you sense something is wrong,
or they are going to raise a stink!

Questions for Reflection and Discussion

1. Some of the traits of a potentially outstanding marriage partner are not readily apparent; they are often noticeable only over time. One of these is the "real ability to work through problems." Being able to work through problems is a sign of growing maturity in the Lord (Eph. 4:13-15; James 1:5-8). Think again about some of the reasons God allows problems to come our way and what the results will be if we do things His way (2 Cor. 1:3-7; James 1:2-4; 1 Pet. 1:6-9). Do you feel that this trait is something you can teach someone after you marry the person? How vital will this trait be in the one you marry? How can you tell when someone depends on his or her own strength and wisdom instead of relying on God?

2. What problems might occur in a Catholic-Protestant marriage or in a charismatic-noncharismatic, Pentecostal-non-Pentecostal marriage. What problems may occur in a Jewish-Christian marriage or with a Christian marrying an atheist, an agnostic or someone in a cult or other religion? Among all these, which marriages do you believe God would be most likely to approve or disapprove? Discuss these problems thoroughly.

3. Reread the section on "Steady Problems." Should adults "go steady"? Is "going steady" appropriate for children or teenagers? Why? Why not? Discuss.

4. Go back over each of the fourteen traits of a potentially good marriage partner. How vital is each trait? Are there some less vital than others? How about the "three more qualities" at the end of the chapter? How vital are they? Write down your answers, then discuss them.

5. Many people seem to take a very casual approach to love and marriage. As a result, they rarely "build their house upon the rock," and heavy storms come along, causing their house to collapse (Matt. 7:24-27). Many Christians also take a very casual approach to God's love and His desire to give them wisdom (James 1:5) and "the mind of Christ" (1 Cor. 2:16) when it comes to making vital decisions such as marriage. Is it because they don't have the confidence that the Lord has their best interest at heart or because they don't want the Lord's answer? Discuss this. Add any other reasons people approach marriage or the Lordship of Christ casually.

Dear Ray,

I'm in a large singles' group at our church. Although the church is Bible-believing, to be honest, the singles' group isn't. It's a lot more social than spiritual. We have a lot of fun, and I've been in the group for more than ten years.

I suppose it happens in all singles' groups: One by one couples pair off, and many marry. I go to all the weddings and even help decorate. At first I was happy when friends said they were going to get married. I looked forward to the day when I'd be getting married too. But, Ray, I'm not sure I'll ever get married now. Not that I couldn't, but I'm not sure I'd say yes to anybody. Suddenly divorce after divorce hits the same couples that looked so great when they said their vows at the altar. Two of the couples have divorced and are dating four other people in our group. That seems strange to me. But strangest of all are these divorces. Why are they happening? Aren't Christians supposed to have great marriages? Or does divorce just follow marriage?

Is there any way you could help me know why so many singles in our church are becoming marriage drop-outs? Thanks.

Single Forever?

*He who finds a (true) wife
finds a good thing,
and obtains favor of the Lord.
Proverbs 18:22, Amplified*

SEVEN

WRONG REASONS FOR GETTING MARRIED

In many weddings
the bride looks stunning,
and the groom looks stunned!

There are many right reasons for getting married. Perhaps the "rightest" is so the two of you can serve Jesus Christ better together than you could if you were single. Secondary reasons include love, companionship, sharing, the strength of prayer when two pray (Matt. 18:19), the joy of rearing children together and the fulfillment of God-blessed sex.

There are also wrong reasons for marrying. I constantly counsel people in deep distress who married for one or more of these wrong reasons. They made a great mistake in marrying, but that doesn't mean their problem can't be solved. They usually didn't know it was a wrong reason at the time they married. Only a fool bangs his or her head with a hammer on purpose.

Let me tell you more about my courtship and engagement to Arlyne.

I first asked Arlyne out as a way to get even with my girlfriend, a college freshman who had stood me up for another guy. Arlyne was a pretty college senior who would soon be leaving the area to teach elementary school, though she hadn't yet signed a contract. My parents adored her.

One day my father said, "Ray, you need to consider getting married. I know you. You're footloose and fancy free. You're dating girls in Los Angeles who are going to get you in trouble."

Dad continued, "Now, take Arlyne. A fine young Christian woman. She's a senior. All her education is paid for. If you marry her, you won't have to pay a nickel. She'll be making big money right from the start. Two teachers, both bringing home a fortune. Imagine it."

"But, Dad," I protested, "I really like this other girl."

Dad cut me off. "That's foolish. If you marry a college freshman, you'll have to put her through college yourself. You can't afford that. Marry Arlyne."

Let me stress that my folks had my best interests at heart. They knew I was one lonely guy. They were worried about what kind of mess I might get myself into. (I lived by my feelings.) They respected Arlyne and saw the Christian she was (and is to this day). They knew she would do well as a teacher, and to them two salaries meant we would be able to live better than they ever had.

After that conversation Mom and Dad launched an Arlyne campaign. Mom made extra-special meals whenever I brought Arlyne to the house. I heard "Arlyne this" and "Arlyne that." My dad was the kind of man who could have sold refrigerators to Eskimos. I got sold. Or rather Arlyne got sold to me. I married my darlin' Arlyne within six months of our first date. Nearly every day for the next twelve years I wanted a divorce — until I discovered what God's Word says about marriage. The rest of the story is *Marriage Plus*!

Social Pressure
Is a Wrong Reason to Marry

Pressure from parents ("You're twenty-four and still single. What's wrong with you?") can be unbearable. Parents who talk about how eager they are to have grandchildren when their own child isn't even married are doing immeasurable harm. Well-meaning married friends who talk about how exciting it is to be married and then say, "I can hardly wait for you to get married too," are putting terrible pressure on a single person. Churches that have couples' retreats with no alternate plan for the singles leave singles wondering, What person can I couple with? I plead with every single: Don't crack under the pressure. "Those who wait for the Lord will gain new strength" (Is. 40:31). Marrying under pressure is like buying under pressure; you're likely to find you brought home the wrong thing.

You'd be amazed at how many similar stories I hear. One familiar pattern goes like this: An engaged person will say, "God has given us a miracle to confirm that we're meant for each other." Or "My parents say we're meant for each other." Or "I feel led that she's the one for me."

I rejoice with these happy couples. I privately pray they've *really* heard from God. But I'm wary, so wary that I've written the following story, a tongue-in-cheek approach to Genesis 24, a passage sometimes used as a model for knowing God's will about marriage.

Let me fill you in on the background behind the biblical story of Isaac finding a wife. After Abraham proved he was willing to obey God to the point of sacrificing his son Isaac (God stopped it from happening), God gave Abraham a magnificent promise:

> Indeed I will greatly bless you, and I will greatly multiply your seed as the stars of the heavens, and as the sand which is on the seashore; and your seed shall possess the gate of their enemies. And in your seed all the nations of the earth shall be blessed, because you have obeyed My voice (Gen. 22:17-18).

Jesus Christ came to us through the fulfillment of this promise.

In Genesis 24 Isaac was of a marrying age. So was Rebekah. But they had a big problem: They were unaware of each other's existence. She lived in Mesopotamia. He lived in Canaan.

But Papa Abraham, a real romantic, decided love was in the air. "Isaac," he said, "you're past puberty. It's time you tied the knot with some fair maiden."

Isaac, no slouch, was turned on by the idea. "But, Dad," he complained, "I've checked out all the girls on the block. They're all losers."

Not to worry. Abraham said, "Son, trust your dad. I've got a servant with a keen eye. I'm going to send him to the land of kissing cousins. He'll bring you back the girl of your dreams."

"Dad, I'm with you all the way. I know your servant scout. I'll marry whomever he picks out. Just remind him that I want a woman who is spiritually alive, who has a lot of money, who is a virgin and who makes me say, 'Va va va voooooom!' "

Vital point 1: Isaac was completely submitted to his father.

The trusted servant got his assignment. After taking an oath of office, he loaded ten camels with treasures any girl would love. Then he cameled his way to a far land. And there she was — Rebekah of Sunnybrook Farm! At first sight the servant prayed, "God, do You see that girl who obviously works out with Stormie Omartian exercise videos? Well, if she's in good enough shape to feed all my camels — if she makes the offer and carries through on it — I'll know it's a sign that she's the right one for Isaac."

Now feeding camels is a sweaty job, one Rebekah would naturally have shunned. After all, this was the desert. These weren't the first camels she'd ever seen. But Rebekah came through; from the well she drew water to satisfy all his camels.

Vital point 2: Rebekah's eagerness to feed the servant's camels (after the servant had prayed for this sign) was a miracle, a sign from God to the servant.

Vital point 3: Rebekah wasn't afraid of work.

Once the work was done, Rebekah took the servant home to meet her parents. Bringing out the gifts, the servant had a long talk with Rebekah's dad. "Listen, I know a young man, the perfect match for your daughter. True, they haven't met yet. But that's just a formality. It will be love at first sight. Trust me."

Rebekah's dad agreed. And, although he would probably never see her again, he wanted her to live happily ever after. Everything was arranged. Rebekah rode into the sunset, waving a fond farewell to Mommy and Daddy.

Vital point 4: Rebekah was totally submitted to her parents.

She turned to the servant and said, "I'm crazy about feeding your camels, and I can't wait to get to Canaan and feed Isaac too."

Genesis 24:67 describes the happy wedding. Isaac married Rebekah, "and he loved her."

Vital point 5: This couple was in love when they married.

Let's summarize the story so far. We have some of the elements of a great marriage: (1) total submission to parents; (2) miracles from the Lord; (3) a hard-working spouse; (4) love.

But was it a great marriage? Here's where most people are in for a surprise. Look at the highlights of the rest of the story. (1) Isaac gave Rebekah to a king's harem, and God supernaturally intervened to get her out (Gen. 26:1-11). (2) Rebekah taught her son Jacob to lie to Isaac (Gen. 27:1-19). (3) Rebekah stirred up such hatred between her sons that Jacob had to run away for many years from Esau's violent anger (Gen. 27:20-45).

Many people want to use Genesis 24 as a model for knowing God's will about marriage, but (1) it's not enough to have a fairy-tale courtship, even if God is in it. Both the husband and the wife have to work at their marriage for "as long as they both shall live" if they want to remain happy. (2) The romance of dating doesn't ensure a happy marriage. The romance has to continue "for as long as they both shall live." (3) Marriage requires more than hard workers who make good salaries. (4) Marriage requires more than parents who just know their child has found the "right one." (5) Marriage requires more than signs from God that "prove" your choice.

Warning: Never marry because of somebody's prophecy, no matter how godly the prophet seems to be. You could end up wanting to stone the prophet! Be careful, too, not to marry just because you or anyone else says, "The Lord told me," or "I felt led."

Marriage requires (1) knowing and living God's Word (Matt. 7:24-27); (2) getting to *know* the person you plan to marry; and (3) some practical thinking that lifts you above feelings.

Pregnancy
Is a Wrong Reason to Marry

A baby is God's vote that He wants the world to continue. A happily married Christian couple can be thrilled when the doctor announces that a baby is on the way. All that changes, however, when the doctor gives that news to an unwed mother.

My year as chaplain for the Salvation Army Booth Home for Unwed Mothers in Oakland, California, in the late sixties is a cherished memory. I counseled with most of the unwed mothers whether they received Christ or not. The terrible guilt; the anger at being abandoned by males who had declared their love; the fear of the future; the frustration and hurt at the anger of the family; being overwhelmed with their own guilt and disappointments — all this was enough to make me realize why God says no couple should have sex outside marriage.

God loves us. He sets rules not to limit our joy — but to assure it. Jesus Christ weeps at human pain even before He heals it (John 11:33-35; 38-44). But so often that pain was avoidable.

What can be done about a pregnancy outside marriage? A woman has four alternatives: (1) marry the father of the baby; (2) keep the baby but remain single; (3) put the baby up for adoption; and (4) abort the baby. As for the fourth option, abortion is murder, forbidden by God. If you are contemplating abortion, please stop. The unborn is a human being in every way (Ps. 139:13-16; Jer. 1:4-5). As Micah 6:7 asks, "Shall I present my first-born for my rebellious acts, the fruit of my body for the sin of my soul?" The answer is no.

If you have had an abortion in the past, please know that Jesus Christ loves you. If you've recognized your sin and confessed it to the Lord, He has forgiven you and "cleansed you from all unrighteousness" (1 John 1:9; see also Rom. 8:1). The repentant Christian can know that she'll see her baby again. [To understand this further, get Jack Hayford's book *I'll Hold You in Heaven: Healing and Hope for the Parent Who Has Lost a Child Through Miscarriage, Stillbirth, Abortion, or Early Infant Death* (Regal Books).]

The words of Christ for all caught in the tragedy of sexual sin are those addressed to an adulteress caught in the very act: "Go your way; from now on sin no more" (John 8:11). Repent, don't repeat.

If a woman is pregnant, is the father responsible to marry her? Is sexual intercourse or pregnancy the act of marriage itself? Is sexual intercourse a private marriage ceremony that can pronounce the couple husband and wife? Are couples who are living together without marriage "married in God's eyes"? God's Word does not indicate the father of the baby is responsible for marrying the mother. God has not said that sexual immorality and marriage are synonymous. From both the Old and New Testaments we see that sex outside marriage does not necessitate marriage.

According to Exodus 22:16-17, "If a man seduces a virgin who is not engaged, and lies with her, he must pay a dowry for her to be his wife. If her father absolutely refuses to give her to him, he shall pay money equal to the dowry for virgins."

One can make too much or too little of this law. It would be too much to say the same rules should be applied today. This was Old Testament law. Under that law the dad owned his daughter. She was his to give away in marriage or to keep. If, for whatever reason, he didn't want to lose his daughter, he simply refused to let her marry. Thank God "you are not under law, but under grace" (Rom. 6:14). The writer of Hebrews tells us that Jesus Christ "is...the mediator of a *better* covenant, which has been enacted on *better* promises" (Heb. 8:6, italics mine).

To make too little of this law would be to miss the mercy in it. This law protected the girl's father, letting him decide whether a marriage should take place; it also protected the girl from being purchased like a slave. Dads generally knew their daughters well. This gave the dad the opportunity to turn down a male who might have been wrong for his daughter. The seduced girl could appeal to her dad, stating her request in the matter.

The major point: Sexual intercourse was not necessarily valid grounds for marriage in the Old Testament.

As for the New Testament, let's look at Hebrews 13:4: "Let marriage be held in honor among all, and let the marriage bed be undefiled; for fornicators and adulterers God will judge."

The Greek word *judge* in Hebrews 13:4 is *krino* and means "to sentence to hell." The Bible is clear. Those who are having sex outside marriage and refuse to repent of it will be judged guilty by God and sent to hell (Rev. 21:8; 22:15). In no way does God consider sexual intercourse to be marriage. The desire for sex may lead to marriage. Sex is a major reason for marriage. But it does not mean that because sexual immorality has occurred there must be a marriage. The false belief that it does has created many heartaches in forced marriages and led to many divorces. Especially sad are forced marriages with unbelievers, marriages that begin by totally violating 2 Corinthians 6:14.

For further insight I recommend Nancy Martin's booklet *Unplanned Pregnancy.*[1] She gives some great counsel for those having to make such vital decisions.

Rebound
Is a Wrong Reason to Marry

Jeremiah 17:9 warns, "The heart is more deceitful than all else and is desperately sick; who can understand it?" That heart of yours can fool you. It wants what it wants when it wants it. Feelings get in the way of God's Word when we let our hearts rule our heads. A classic case of this is rebound.

Here's the scenario: A previous love interest terminates a relationship. The one cut off launches a frantic attempt to prove he or she is still desirable. It is an "I'll show them" action that usually leads to disaster. The game plan almost always backfires.

A good rule of thumb is: Do not ask someone to marry you or accept an invitation to marry within eighteen months of being hurt in the break-up of a serious romantic relationship.

Escape or Rebellion
Is a Wrong Reason to Marry

Using marriage as an escape route from an unhappy home life is usually a one-way ticket from the frying pan into the fire.

When adults remain angry with at least one parent, they tend to fixate on one or more of that parent's sins, faults or bad habits. They are so angered by that sin, fault or habit that, once married, they transfer that negative emotion to their spouses. Whenever the spouse does anything that remotely reminds the bitter person of the unforgiven parent, he or she will explode with anger. In time, at least subconsciously, this person comes to think of the spouse and the parent as being the same person; the spouse may be doing very little to incur the bitter person's wrath, and yet wrath remains.

If a person marries in rebellion to his or her parents, the pent-up anger and bitterness will come out in the marriage. Any continued anger or bitterness will quickly fray the joy of that marriage and make it far less than it should be.

I highly recommend three books to help you or someone you are dating better understand family backgrounds: Kevin Leman's *The Birth Order Book* (Dell Publishers); Kevin Leman and Randy Carlson's *Unlocking the Secrets of Your*

Childhood Memories (Pocket Books) and Tim LaHaye's *You and Your Family* (Family Life Seminars).

Feeling Lonely or Incomplete
Is a Wrong Reason to Marry

I know many healthy, mature Christian singles who are having the time of their lives. They take art classes and drama classes, read books, enjoy their jobs, baby-sit for married friends and cook feasts for their friends. Their lives are rich and full. Often these people work in church-related projects or ministry. Loneliness doesn't seem to be a problem to them.

Yet the number-one complaint I hear from singles is, "I'm lonely." Not everyone is lonely for the same reasons. Many feel isolated not because other singles don't exist within their social circle, but because they maintain only superficial relationships; holding everyone at arm's length, they are close to no one. They may give gifts to others, but they never give themselves.

Some people pull away from relationships because they believe they are unlikable, certainly unlovable. They find it hard to trust God's love, let alone any human love. Some people would be less lonely if they learned the social graces described in chapter 5.

In some cases an emotional dictatorship keeps a lonely person bound. A mother, father or friend holds an unhealthy control over them. Often Christian forgiveness, writing loving letters (in spite of what they write back), and an absolute break from this kind of situation are needed for healing to occur.

Another kind of loneliness is because of our mobile society or the changing seasons of life. When a single person moves to a new city or state, starts attending a new school or gets a new job, he or she has to form new relationships. Real relationships take time to form. Loneliness fills the gap of time between "hello" and becoming buddies.

Some singles are lonely simply because they have not yet met the partner God is preparing for them. Relax — God does things only "in the fulness of the time" (Gal. 4:4).

If you are separated, divorced or widowed, you most likely feel very lonely. And lonely people are too often vulnerable people. It is easier to take advantage of a hurting, lonely person — in so much pain that even poison ointment may seem soothing for a while.

There are two wrong choices a person can make: (1) stay locked within the loneliness and do nothing about it, becoming a prisoner in a solitary cell; or (2) stay locked within the loneliness by reaching out for the *wrong* love. As George Washington said, "It is better to be alone than in bad company." Giving your body in an attempt to feel loved leaves a lonely sin-hangover. "Relationship at any price" is as dangerous and ignorant as "peace at any price."

If you're a Christian, Christ is the center of your identity. He wants to flood you with joy. It's unfair to hold a man or woman responsible for keeping you happy or feeling secure. What if he or she suddenly died? Does that mean all your contentment would be gone? Never hold another person responsible for what only Christ can give.

Marriage won't make you happier. Once you marry, you will be as happy as you are within yourself now from day to day, when nothing very exciting is happening. A wedding, no matter how beautiful, is over in a flash, and the wedding gown gets replaced with reality. After the honeymoon you have to settle down to happiness with bad breath, bills, endless work and disagreements that never rose while you were dating.

Physical Appearance
Is a Wrong Reason to Marry

Nothing proves the old adage "Beauty is only skin deep" better than a high school or college reunion. People gain weight, grow wrinkles, get bald.

You may say, "I know my beauty is fading. So shouldn't I get married now before things get worse?" No. Your looks or somebody else's looks are terrible reasons for marriage. Blaise Pascal said, "If a man loves a woman for her beauty, does he love her? No. For the smallpox, which destroys her beauty without killing her, causes his love to cease." Remember, the finest music is played on the oldest violins.

If you marry him because he's handsome, if you marry her because she's gorgeous, you are headed for a shock. Though some men and women do keep their looks, it doesn't happen often. One tragic trip through the front windshield of a car or a diagnosis of some dreadful disease, and one begins to know why marriage has to mean much more than looks.

Divorcing someone because he or she looks older is like divorcing someone because he or she breathes. Aging and breath are vital parts of life.

Guilt or Pity
Is a Wrong Reason to Marry

There is nothing wrong in marrying someone who has a handicap or physical disability if you really love this person and if you're both certain your love will last a lifetime in spite of the hurdles. But no one who is thinking straight wants to be married for pity — instead of love. Just as no one should marry for good looks, no one should marry because of bad looks. If you feel sorry for the one you marry, you will end up having people feel sorry for you and your spouse.

If you are considering marrying someone physically limited by a handicap, are you absolutely certain you are willing to accept that handicap as if it were your own, without complaint? Will you live joyfully within its limits for the rest of your life? If someone of the opposite sex came along after you were married, someone with an equally great personality but healthy and physically complete in every way, would you stay faithful to your spouse? Or would you believe you married the wrong person? Would you complain to God about it? Would you divorce?

If you are handicapped and your spouse met someone like the person described above, would you become jealous and fearful? What if you saw your spouse and this person enjoying rich communication with each other? Would you be afraid of losing your spouse? Also, are you willing to let your spouse help you and take care of you? Or have you developed an inflexible, independent spirit? What if you marry and a spouse disrupts your routine? How do you feel about others interrupting your routine or trying to help you now?

I have met happily married couples where one or both were handicapped. But they did not marry because one pitied the other. They married because they loved each other and answered all of the above questions thoughtfully and honestly with a positive response. Can you?

Sexual Attraction
Is a Wrong Reason to Marry

Engagement is often an urge on the verge of a merge. I told you about my quick courtship of Arlyne. There was another motivating force behind my marriage to her. My libido. I had a sex drive that was never in neutral.

When we started dating, Arlyne made it clear there would be no hanky-panky before marriage. The more I tried to change her mind, the more she took her stand. Guys seldom marry what they can get for nothing. Her price tag for sex was marriage. So I married her — as soon as possible.

God understands sexual attraction. "But because of immoralities, let each man have his own wife, and let each woman have her own husband" (1 Cor. 7:2). It will and should be one of the major reasons for marrying someone. But it must not be *the* reason.

If you are considering marriage to someone, and the two of you *don't* struggle with your sex drives, you may have a serious problem. Either you are not in love at all, or at least one of you has no natural sex drive. If that sex drive is missing in you both, you may have a sexless marriage, something almost nonexistent in healthy marriages. If just one of you has virtually no sex drive, and the other doesn't discover this until marriage, the one with a normal sex drive will be highly frustrated in the marriage. If you sense this is a problem, the two of you should talk together with a godly Christian counselor. If either of you realizes the other one won't satisfy your sexual need after marriage, break off the relationship.

God wants married couples to have a great sex life. In fact, 1 Corinthians 7:5 analyzed boils down to: Great sex in marriage will stop Satan from being able to tempt either the husband or the wife with anyone else.

However, marrying so that you can have sex with someone isn't enough to ensure a great marriage. Nearly a hundred percent of married couples have sex after they're married, and yet over a million couples a year bail out of their marriages — in spite of sex. The second major reason for divorce in America today is sexual unfaithfulness, and the fourth major reason is sexual incompatibility. If sex were the great "end all and be all" of marriage, no one would ever get divorced.

Sex will be extremely important in marriage, but it won't take much time in the average day. The couple who is hot and heavy in their date life is going to face a terrible realism once they marry. Sex at its best becomes a wonderful but not daily event. Sex at its worst becomes something at least one spouse wants to avoid.

Someone is bound to ask, "You list sexual incompatibility as the fourth major reason for divorce. Wouldn't it make good sense for a couple to have sex before marriage so they can find out how compatible they might be?" In their book *Givers, Takers, and Other Kinds of Lovers*, Josh McDowell and Paul Lewis answer that question.

> Let me give you an example of how some guys think. A problem develops in his relationship with a woman and the first thing the guy wants to do is go to bed. Why? Because he believes, "If I can please my mate physically, the problem, no matter what it is, will take care of itself." Usually, the woman doesn't want the man to touch her until the problem is talked out. Sex is the last thing she wants. That doesn't deter a lot of men, however. And they begin to pressure the woman until she gives in. As a result, she develops negative attitudes toward sex. This is why I stress the fact that unless you develop the spiritual and soulish dimensions of your lives, you're going to rob yourself and your mate in the area of your physical relationship.[2]

God doesn't say no to sex outside marriage because He's trying to be a spoil-sport or prude. He says no so that you'll enjoy maximum sex once you're married. To accept less than that is to accept less than God's best for you.

"He or She Loves Me"
Is a Wrong Reason to Marry

Love that turns into marriage has to be mutual. Both of you have to vote the other "The Person I'd Most Like to Spend the Rest of My Life With." If only one of you thinks that way, there should be no marriage.

As the song says, a lot of people "fall in love with love." Check your heart carefully when you find it pounding. It may not be love at all. Don't act on your feelings, but on God's Word.

"I Wanted to Marry, and He or She Was There"
Is a Wrong Reason to Marry

I hear it often: "I married because he or she was handy and available." This is usually said by someone who was desperate to marry. He proposed. She accepted. Often one or both will add, "I knew all along we shouldn't get married, but we did."

Your chances at getting a great husband or wife by simply getting married because you want to *be* married are about equal to winning the lottery. In fact, it's more like playing Russian roulette with six bullets in the gun. Spin the chamber, and bang!

"I Didn't Want to Hurt Her Feelings"
Is a Wrong Reason to Marry

There came a point when I knew I shouldn't marry Arlyne, but I didn't want to hurt her feelings. Three days before our wedding date, I finally worked up the nerve to call it off. I was coming to my senses. No, I didn't want to spend the rest of my life in a boxing ring with a woman who told me all my faults.

I drove to her apartment, walked up the stairs and rang the doorbell, determined to end our engagement. I would have done it too, except she looked so beautiful when she answered the door. Seeing me, her face lit up, and she said, "Oh, honey, come in. We have more wedding presents!" I reluctantly walked in and watched her unwrap treasures "for our home." I stood there and thought, I *can't* break up with her. The wedding invitations have been out for a month. People are coming from all over the country. They've already bought gifts. Most of all, I can't hurt Arlyne's feelings. So I married her and broke her heart for the first twelve years of our marriage.

God did prove faithful to His promise in Romans 8:28. He "worked good" out of our marriage, basically because in spite of her constant tears Arlyne prayed a lot for me. She stayed in the marriage, prayed and waited for me to be saved and remain faithful.

An inscription could be written over our marriage: "And as for you [devil], you meant evil against [us], but God meant it for good in order to bring about this present result, to preserve many people alive" (Gen. 50:20). Going through the pain of those first twelve years of my marriage, how could I have known God was allowing me to identify with the agony of the worst of marriages so He could give hurting people the same thing I have now — a great one.

A Word to the Wise

To never marry because there might be problems would be like running from all human relationships because there might be problems. Don't kid yourself. The human element in *all* close relationships means there *will* be problems from time to time. No matter how wonderful the person you marry, there *will* be problems. But you'll have problems if you stay single too.

But always remember: If something inside you is telling you *not* to marry a certain person, pray! Ask the Lord if He is speaking to you. The devil can lie to you (John 8:44) and try to steal your joy and squelch God's perfect plan for you. But "greater is He who is in you than he who is in the world" (1 John 4:4). If you continue to *know* you shouldn't marry someone, don't. God can make Himself heard only if you'll listen and obey.

He said, "If you refuse to marry me, I'll die."
Sure enough, seventy years later he died!

Questions for Reflection and Discussion

1. Why do you suppose Rebekah would have fed all of the camels of Abraham's servant and his team? Could there have been any other reason aside from its being a direct sign from God in answer to the servant's prayer? Discuss any *dangers* that might exist in using signs or direct prophecy from someone to select a marriage partner.

2. Think through the major points in Genesis 24. Do you know any couples who seemed in every way to be "right" for each other, yet their marriage turned out to be a disaster? What went wrong? As a single Christian, what lessons can you learn from this story?

3. If a couple is well-matched in every other way, but one of them can seemingly serve Christ better if he or she is single rather than married, should the couple marry? Reverse this situation: Suppose they seemingly can serve Christ better married to each other than by remaining single but don't seem well-matched. Should they marry? Why? Why not? How do you believe Christ Himself would view either situation? Discuss this.

4. Rebellion is a wrong reason for doing anything, including getting married. Read 1 Samuel 15:23, Jeremiah 28:16-17 and Hebrews 12:15. What happens when rebellion takes hold and a "root of bitterness" springs up? Discuss how this root could be dangerous to a marriage.

5. Since God invented sex (Gen. 2:24-25), why do you suppose He commanded it not to be entered into except in marriage (Heb. 13:4)? List all the reasons you can think of. Discuss this.

Dear Ray,

   I've just read your book *Marriage Plus*. It's great. It's the first time I've had a real picture of the beautiful thing God planned marriage to be. But I'll never get married. My folks fought until my mom quit their marriage. My friends' folks fight just like my folks did. Every guy I go out with wants to paw me or wants me to make love. I'm sick of the single life, but I never want to get married. Why put yourself through the torture of being married to someone who doesn't really love you anyway? Pretty soon you won't love him either. Besides, *love* is a meaningless word. That's what I think, anyway. What do you think?

Fed Up

Many waters cannot quench
the flame of love,
neither can the floods drown it.
If a man tried to buy it
with everything he owned,
he couldn't do it.
          Song of Solomon 8:7, LB

EIGHT

WHAT IS
REAL LOVE?

Love is what makes two people
sit in the middle of a bench
when there's plenty of room at both ends.

S adly, the word *love* is used far too frequently today. In the course of a day we might hear someone say, "I love ice cream." "I love my dog." "I love you." Does that person feel the same way about each of these three things? On a first date, one person may say to the other, "I love you." If totally honest, that person might mean, "I lust you." Or maybe "I'm deeply infatuated with you." But real love takes time to develop.

One of my favorite Ann Landers columns is a list that points out the differences between real love and infatuation. If you think that you're really in love, study these definitions:

Love or Infatuation?

Infatuation leaps into bloom. Love usually takes root slowly and grows with time.

Infatuation is accompanied by a sense of uncertainty. You are stimulated and thrilled but not really happy. You are miserable when (he or she) is absent. You can't wait until you see (him or her) again.

Love begins with a feeling of security. You are warm with a sense of (his or her) nearness. Even when (he or she) is away, miles do not separate you. You want (him or her) near. But near or far, you know (he or she) is yours, and you can wait.

Infatuation says, "We must get married right away. I can't risk losing (him or her)."

Love says, "Don't rush into anything." You are sure of one another. You can plan your future with confidence.

Infatuation has an element of sexual excitement. If you are honest, you will discover it's difficult to enjoy one another unless you know it will lead to intimacy.

Love is the maturation of friendship. You must be friends before you can be lovers.

Infatuation lacks confidence. When (he or she) is away, you wonder if (he or she) is with another. Sometimes you even check.

Love means trust. You may fall into infatuation. But you never fall into love. Infatuation might lead you to do things for which you might be sorry. But love never will.

Love leads you up. It makes you look up. It makes you think up. It makes you a better person than you were before.[1]

Still More Differences Between Infatuation and Love

Infatuation is often something only one person feels. The other person may not know — or care to know — about it. How many thirteen-year-old girls are infatuated with Tom Cruise? Do you think he cares? Infatuation is fickle and changes with age or with meeting someone else.

Real love, on the other hand, requires an exchange of hearts after much time. The two must know and enjoy each other's personality so well that they are "knit together in love" (Col. 2:2).

Infatuation keeps someone's head in the clouds, thinking of the other person morning, noon and night. Church, work, school — anything becomes far more difficult if the other person is not present. If you're infatuated, you would rather be alone with this person than in a group, because you like having him or her all to yourself and don't like sharing him or her with anyone else. Your biggest dream is to be as passionate as possible with this person.

Love keeps both feet on the ground. Thinking of the other person gives great joy. Every memory of being together brings real pleasure and no guilt. Church, work, school — all become even more meaningful, as you want to grow and be all you can be to bring greater blessings to the one you love. You are proud of your loved one. You enjoy being in a crowd together, because others can see how fine a person he or she is. Passion can wait for marriage, because you both are secure in the other's love.

Infatuation keeps you nervous, hoping you'll receive the approval of the one you're crazy over. You're self-conscious and afraid you may do something dumb and embarrassing. Unless you are a chatterbox, it is sometimes hard to think of things to say.

Love is relaxed and comfortable. You talk freely and "[speak] the truth in love" (Eph. 4:15). You pray together, study the Bible together, laugh and even cry together without embarrassment. If one does something dumb, you both have a good laugh, without self-consciousness.

Infatuation dresses to attract the eyes of the other. You are not interested in wearing clothes appropriate for an occasion, but to seduce. You cling to the other person and never want to let go. You like to touch and kiss as often as possible whether alone or in a crowd — to be reassured of the other's love.

Love dresses appropriately for any occasion. You care, but are never worried, about how you look. You enjoy looking good for the one you love. You are content talking or holding hands. Being sure of each other's love, you don't need to kiss in front of others or continually reassure each other with touches. Even when alone, you never offend each other or God with actions.

Infatuation concentrates on and talks about the other's eyes, hair, figure, car, money, material possessions, ability to kiss.... You love to share with friends every detail of the latest date. You make excuses for any flaws in the other person's character. You make up stories to impress friends or parents.

Love concentrates and talks about the other's faith, prayer life, love for God, kindness, tenderness, empathy, sense of humor.... You don't have to be talking about the other person all the time, but you don't hide your relationship. You don't make up excuses about flaws, but accept them, with no dreams of changing them. You would never lie for the one you love, though that person never puts you in such a position.

Infatuation dreams about the future and feels any time away from the other is wasted. One of your biggest surprises is that a summer away from your love causes your feelings to fade or stop.

Love causes two people to map out the future together. Your plans may keep you in the same place, or you may have to spend time apart preparing for the future, maybe in school or in missions. Your plans are realistic, and you can trust each other together or apart. You would be willing to give the other up if God intervened or showed one of you the marriage wasn't right.

Though many great relationships begin as infatuation and grow into love, the difference between the two is like night and day.

Marry only someone you love.

Four Kinds of Love

The Bible defines love and infatuation by both example and definition. For example, Amnon was infatuated with Tamar until he raped her (2 Sam. 13:1-14). "Then Amnon hated her" (v. 15).

On the other hand, Joseph, Christ's earthly stepfather, obviously loved Mary. Before he understood she was pregnant through the Holy Spirit and not by a man, he thought what most guys would think if their girlfriend was pregnant, and not by them. In anger and humiliation he could have "disgraced her," but "being a righteous man, and not wanting to disgrace her, [he] desired to put her away secretly" (Matt. 1:19). He wanted to end their relationship without making her a public scandal. That's love.

As for New Testament definitions, they are much clearer in the original Greek than they are in most of our English translations. The Greeks used four different words for *love* to designate what they meant. Our English interpretations have generally gone back to the one word *love*. The four Greek words are *eros*, *phileo*, *storge* and *agape*.

Agape was a word Jesus Christ created to express the highest form of love. You can't find it in any secular first-century Greek writings; yet it's used 116 times in the Greek New Testament. Only Christians can fully release *agape*, which is a "fruit of the Spirit" (Gal. 5:22) received when one is born again. We can release it to others because it is within us. Paul explains, "The love of God has been poured out within our hearts through the Holy Spirit who was given to us" (Rom. 5:5). *Agape* is self-sacrificing, without any self-centeredness or selfishness. Coming from God, it results in doing only godly things. From the human level, it puts Christ first and cares about everyone. *Agape* and sin cannot exist together at the same time.

Why *Agape* Is Essential for Godly *Eros*

The Greek word *eros* was originally a beautiful word describing wholesome, shameless passion in marriage. Any strong and fulfilling marriage will include great passion between two lovers committed to each other for a lifetime.

Today, the word *eros* — or erotic — is an unredeemed word used to express pornography of every kind. *Agape* is absolutely necessary for the word *eros* to be returned to the godly place our Lord intended it to occupy. If we cannot change our nation, we can at least keep ourselves from entertaining sexual sin. Fleshly resolution is not enough; we need Christ's *agape* love working in us, calling us to Himself.

Why *Agape* Is Essential for Godly *Storge*

Storge, or family love, is used by Paul in Romans 12:10: "Be devoted to one another in brotherly love."

The word *storge* brings forth the cry of the Three Musketeers, "All for one and one for all." It prompts men and women to defend their country and their homes. It is an instinctive love for one's own family, the kind of love you should have for your brothers and sisters in Christ. I've heard people say they were embarrassed to admit they watched "Little House on the Prairie." They called the familial love portrayed corny and unreal. God doesn't agree. He put that kind of family love within each human. That program had such high ratings because the world sees so little of that kind of love, which is strong only when it is undergirded with *agape*: I love you no matter what you do.

I see *storge* evident in Jesus' concern for His family — His mother — even as He suffered beyond imagination, hanging on a cross.

Whom do you think about when you are suffering? Is your life a witness to your parents, your family? Do you exemplify the love of Christ? If you're living away from them, do you phone home to express your love? If you can't afford to reach out and touch them by phone, do you write regularly? If you live in the same city, do you visit frequently and invite them to your place? Do you thank your mom and dad for all they've done for you — paying your bills, feeding you, keeping a roof over your head as you were growing up? How you relate to your parents will affect the way you respond to your husband or wife if you ever marry.

Why *Agape* Is Essential for Godly *Phileo*

Phileo has the basic problem of being self-interested. It wants what it wants when it wants it. It gives to get. It is a fragile love, often built on the human senses:

sight ("Wow, she's gorgeous!"), touch ("Your skin is so smooth"), taste ("Your lips taste so good!"), smell ("I love your perfume!") and sound ("That music is so romantic"). It is the very essence of infatuation. *Phileo* must graduate to *agape* if it is to be trusted through thick and thin, which is what marriage is all about.

Agape is absolutely essential to a Christian marriage. If *phileo* is all a couple has going for them, it is easy for one or the other to find someone else more attractive when a spouse grows older.

Agape in Action

While I was ministering in New Zealand in 1977, a thirteen-year-old boy was accused of murdering a six-year-old girl. What would you expect to be the normal response of the parents of the six-year-old? Here's what the girl's father said:

> Because of our own sorrow, we believed we had some idea of what that boy's family must be feeling. I asked Inspector Dalzier, who has given us such wonderful support and understanding, if I could talk to these people. Before long, there we were, tears all around. They realized I had come with no recriminations. I told them I had come just to let them know my wife and I knew how they felt. Captain Davis prayed and that put the seal on what for all of us were sacred moments.[2]

That's *agape* love. Can you imagine what it would be like if every marriage had the love of Christ, the quick ability to forgive the unforgivable, the power to turn others toward God as this couple did?

During the Singles Plus seminar I ask: What if your boyfriend or girlfriend found someone who really would make him or her a *better* lifetime partner than you? In spite of the pain of loss you would feel, would you be *glad* for him or her? Would you encourage him or her to choose the *better*? Or would you hurry and get married if you could so that you wouldn't lose your love? That might take some real heart-searching before you could answer it honestly. But the answer will tell you how much you really love someone.

Dating steadily — being engaged — at least a year before you marry tests your ability to love that person. If you don't pass the test, don't marry the person.

**Many people who think
they have been bitten by the love bug
suddenly realize it was only a louse!**

Questions for Reflection and Discussion

1. Write an answer to the letter preceding chapter 8. How would you minister to this young woman?

2. Reread the definitions of "love" and "infatuation" in this chapter. Why is it so easy to think a person is "in love" when he or she is only "infatuated"? Discuss each of these definitions thoroughly. Add your own insight.

3. Reread the section that defines the four kinds of love. Why is it so important to balance each with *agape*? Discuss how each would either fit or not fit into a dating situation; a marriage.

4. Many people don't seem to feel God's love and thus conclude God doesn't love them. But Romans 8:38-39 and 1 John 4:19 tell us *God's love* is much more than *feeling*; it is a *constant action*. The Lord commands all Christians to "put on love" (Col. 3:14) and to "love your enemies" (Luke 6:27). Will you necessarily feel love for them at the moment? How can your actions and attitude reflect that you love someone even when you may not feel it in your heart? Discuss this.

5. Some Christians believe that once they are saved they will automatically have agape love and all the other "fruit of the Spirit" (Gal. 5:22-23). They grow extremely frustrated when they don't have it. But does this fruit come naturally or must it be developed as we grow in our walk with Christ? According to John 15:4-5 and Hebrews 5:13-14, what must we do to produce "much fruit"? Discuss this.

145

Dear Ray,

Wow! I really enjoyed your Singles Plus seminar. I took so many notes and learned so much. Thanks for teaching it. Now the big news: I think I'm getting married a year from now. Bill proposed last night. I'm trying to keep both feet on the ground, but I really am in love. Everybody, including my folks, thinks Bill is the best guy I've ever dated. So do I. But I'm writing because I love Jesus Christ even more than I love Bill. How can I be sure that Bill is the right husband for me, and I'm the right wife for him? I accepted his proposal, but I've got one little doubt corner in my brain like a yellow light at a traffic signal. It's just caution, not stop. Would you help me? What do I need to think about during the year before I become a Mrs.? How would I know to break up if it really wasn't God's will but just my loving heart? How would Bill know to do the same thing? Hope you can come to our wedding.

A Year From Marriage (Most Likely!)

*And who is the man that is
engaged to a woman and
has not married her?
Let him depart and return to
his house, lest he die
in the battle and
another man marry her.*
                    Deuteronomy 20:7

NINE

THE ENGAGEMENT ARRANGEMENT

*An engagement ring is a tourniquet
applied to the third finger of a woman's left hand
to cut off circulation.*

Deuteronomy 20:7 illustrates the love of God. Today's professional military can scarcely imagine this scene: God is ordering troops home from war so they can marry the ones they left behind. The Christ who celebrates at weddings (John 2:1-11) is this same God; He is love itself (1 John 4:8). He longs to be the One in charge of engagements, weddings *and* marriage. Those who invite Him to all three have the greatest happiness in marriage.

Love is a commitment, and when a man says and means "I love you," his next words should be, "Will you marry me?"

Michael Zadig wrote about his pre-Christian experience of living with a girl without marrying her in an article called "Marriage: Who Needs It?":

> You can't say to someone, "I love you. Let's live together to see what happens." On those terms, either of you can split at a moment's notice. As a result, you never really can be yourself or feel free to disagree without the fear of losing the other person. You can never have the liberty to share your deepest feelings. You have to hold back. The relationship doesn't get a chance to grow because it's based on a conditional acceptance which is the cover for the self-gratification of two people indulging themselves in what they politely term "a meaningful relationship." Real commitment on the other hand says, "I am willing to spend my life with you to see you grow." Love may have some cold spots, and it alone will never be enough to hold two people together. It's commitment that carries them over difficult times. Commitment is what God intended between a man and a woman. That is why He set up marriage — to express a life-long commitment.[1]

What is vital in a marriage proposal and engagement period?

Financial Freedom and Responsibility

> But if anyone does not provide for *his* own, and especially for those of *his* household, *he* has denied the faith, and is worse than an unbeliever (1 Tim. 5:8, italics mine).

God has called every husband to be his wife's provider. The man is responsible for the financial security of the home. First Timothy 5:8 is not referring to a man temporarily out of work and honestly searching for a job. Nor to a man who is sick or handicapped and has his family on welfare. The verse addresses the husband who expects his wife to get a job to support him or to make ends meet. It refers to the husband who is abandoning his children to whatever or whomever while he forces their mom out of the house to get a job.

What does that mean in terms of wedding preparation?

It is still a tradition for the family of the bride to pay for the wedding if they can afford to do so. However, weddings are so expensive — average cost: $3,500 (many weddings are far more costly) — that many families *can't* afford it. Divorce or death may mean the father isn't available to help with this responsibility. Many marrying couples combine their money today to pay for the wedding and often the honeymoon, too. This is fine if (1) they don't spend everything they have.

Pawning wedding presents is tacky. Saying, "God will provide," is true only if the husband has a good job and a strong savings account; and (2) it doesn't start a habit.

A man's marriage proposal should include this declaration: "I have all the money necessary to provide a good place for us to live alone together. I have a good job that will provide for us both. You won't have to be employed unless you want to be. If you decide you want employment, we will put everything you make into savings or buy items to improve our apartment or house or give that money to God. That way, when a baby comes, you can concentrate on being a homemaker and mother. I have an excellent record for keeping my bills paid on time."

Anything less than that financial commitment puts a new marriage in an extreme risk category. Financial collapse is the third-rated reason for divorce.

There is nothing wrong with the bride's contributing to the household start-up costs from her savings. But the poor beginning of a marriage can keep her forced into constant slave labor forever while the couple struggles financially. (To understand this, read the chapter called "The Mom Bomb" from my book *Marriage Plus*.)

A man who borrows money, even from his parents, to pay for his wedding, honeymoon, apartment, furniture, appliances or anything else is making a huge mistake. So is the woman who marries him. Remember Proverbs 22:7, "The rich rules over the poor, and the borrower becomes the lender's slave." Don't fall in debt to your parents. It will obligate you to "slaveship"!

Remember: Two can live as cheaply as one only if one doesn't eat! You may think you can live on love, but your landlord doesn't agree! Living with parents after a couple marries violates Ephesians 5:31: "For this cause [marriage] a man shall leave his father and mother, and shall cleave to his wife; and the two shall become one flesh." The only reason Ephesians 5:31 doesn't mention a wife leaving her parents is because the Ephesian readers already knew a wife always left her parents. Among the people of that day a common phrase for getting married was "to take a wife." (One wife told me, "I know I sure got *taken* when I got married!")

Tragically, many couples have found it isn't "Till death do us part," but "Till debts do us part." You are not ready to marry until you can afford it financially.

The Question of Family and Blessing

Honor your father and mother (which is the first commandment with a promise), that it may be well with you, and that you may live long on the earth (Eph. 6:2-3).

Few moments will ever equal the joy Arlyne and I shared the day our oldest son, Tim, brought the woman he loves, Kelly, to ask us, "Dad and Mom, I believe God has brought Kelly and me together. We would like to be married a year from now. But we want to know: Is there anything either of you sees in us that would stop us from being God's best for each other?" The honor we felt in such trust was a rich reward for parenting. We spent more than an hour confirming Tim's choice and then praying together. We told them we were delighted. I suggested we get together for dinner at least monthly during their engagement. We did. We still get together often. That was more than five years ago. Recently they told us we are going to be grandparents. The extension of a bonded Christian family is one of the greatest witnesses of Christ's love a human can see or know.

Tim and Kelly also went to her parents with the same request. Kelly's dad, the Rev. Jim Nelson, is a counselor at Church on the Way. Diane, her mom, has helped to oversee many church weddings. What a risk our kids took! They knew both Jim and I have repeatedly counseled against certain marriages. We would have spoken out if we had seen something that would have made them a poor match. But our kids trusted the Lord through us. In spite of their feelings, they would rather have not married than to have done so out of God's will.

If both of you have Christian parents, you are blessed. Even if your parents are not Christians, they no doubt care that you succeed in life. Before you get engaged, seek their blessing on your marriage. If they saw something in your intended partner that you didn't see, wouldn't you want to know about it? If not, why not? They may know you better than you know yourself. True, you risk their disapproval by asking them to comment honestly on your marital plans, but their evaluation couldn't be purchased by the best of counselors who don't know the two of you intimately.

I'm sometimes asked, "But what if my parents are dead?" Or "What if my parents are atheists who would never approve of my marrying a Christian? How would I ever get their blessing?" Sadly, there are exceptions that would disqualify or make impossible the parental blessing. But if your parents are available, try to get their blessing. I know of atheist parents who were so impressed by their children's request that the parents became Christians on the spot. Whatever the result, your loving attempt to relate to your family will be a witness to them. Later they may come to Christ because they saw His love through you.

To understand the value of marital blessings from your parents and friends, read *The Blessing* by Gary Smalley and John Trent (Thomas Nelson) and *The Family Blessing* by Rolf Garborg (Word).

If it is impossible to go to your parents and seek their blessing, ask your closest friends who are mature Christians. Ask them to give both of you an honest response to the question, Do you see anything in us that would stop us from being

God's best for each other?

Whether you ask the question of parents or friends, prepare yourself for the occasion with prayer, asking the Lord to speak through these people. Listen to what they say; expect to hear the Lord. Obey Him. The strong disapproval of parents or close Christian friends usually indicates something is wrong with your marriage plans. Thank your parents or friends; never respond in anger or hold a grudge. Unless the problems are minor flaws either of you can work on and change, do not get engaged or married. Never marry without the approval of those who love the Lord and you.

A word about in-laws: In many ways you don't marry only a husband or a wife. You marry his or her parents too. Nearly all parents will play an important part in your lives from the wedding on. Be sure you like the kind of influence they have and feel the relationship between your betrothed and his or her parents is healthy. If either parent dominates their son or daughter before the wedding, that same controlling spirit will be hard for your husband or wife to break after the wedding. Before you marry, get to know your future in-laws.

Don't privately entertain the thought that you will move to another city and take your husband or wife away from domineering parents. Your spouse may not want to leave. Discuss these family matters and act in love toward each other and your parents.

Most in-laws are not outlaws. Studies show that in-laws are great blessings to most marriages — friends, baby-sitters and trustworthy advisers. On the other hand, a poor relationship with close relatives is one of the major reasons given for divorce. Remember: To honor your parents means "to greatly value" them. Honor them so that it will be well with you.

The Test of Time

Those who wait for the Lord will gain new strength (Is. 40:31).

The best engagements last no less than one year and no more than two years. Why? An engagement that lasts less than one year doesn't give you time to know each other well enough to be certain you want to spend the rest of your lives together.

There is precedent for this. In biblical times a betrothal of one year was *not* the hundred-yard dash to the altar so many couples run today. It was a time of getting to know each other's spirit and soul, not each other's body.

A typical Jewish couple of the first century was chosen for each other by the parents, often aided by a professional matchmaker. Though the selection was often made while both candidates were still babies, the reputation of that young person as he or she grew up was very important. Often the young people did not know who had been chosen for them until they were betrothed *exactly one year* before their wedding. When the parental choices were announced, they both had one opportunity to refuse the match. (That rarely happened.) From the moment of their betrothal they were considered husband and wife, although they had no sexual contact until their wedding night.

Engagement, a time of discovery, is meant to settle every heavy doubt. It exposes any serious flaws that may never have surfaced until this important year — flaws that can still be worked out. Unlike the ancient betrothal, if problems aren't worked through, there is still time to call things off. It is NOT legally binding.

Why should the engagement not last more than two years? Engagement is like checking an important book out of the library. The book is out of circulation until you return it. If a man goes steady or gets engaged to a woman in her mid-twenties, he keeps her out of circulation for several years. If he then decides she's not the one for him, he is nothing but a thief. Each year added because of his callousness lessens her probabilities of marriage and adds to her fears.

A lengthy exclusive relationship also presents undue sexual temptation. A kiss no longer satisfies. Sex becomes easy. The acceptance of sexual sin often replaces whatever walk with Christ the two have known previously. Unacceptable excuses and lies replace faith and joy in the Lord, or the one who senses the greatest conviction of guilt will break up the relationship.

Just as with going steady, another problem of long courtships is that familiarity does breed contempt. When an adult couple spends more than two years together without marriage, he may begin using her instead of really caring about her.

If you're caught in this trap of being used, or you realize you're using somebody this way, it's time to wake up.

From her side, familiarity can also breed contempt. Some women nag or order the man around as if he were already a henpecked husband. If he is a Willie Wimp, he'll jump through her hoop. Otherwise he'll growl and bark because he's beginning to live a dog's life. Stop! Isn't there enough mental torture in this world already? Don't add to it by falling into the unhappy-marriage trap while you're still single. Either recognize you're not meant for each other or get some vital Christian counseling and solve your problems together. Put your engagement on hold while you get the counseling. Don't marry until you've spent at least a year without either of you taking the other for granted.

In summary, after one year of Christ-centered courtship, a happy couple should spend the next few months making wedding plans, preparing for marriage.

Personal Preparation

When Arlyne and I went for pastoral counseling prior to our wedding, the pastor asked, "Do you love each other?" We both nodded yes. He immediately began to discuss the wedding plans. That was the extent of our marriage counseling. As you plan to marry, be certain the pastor does a more adequate job, asking probing questions that you answer honestly.

Jack Hayford at the Church on the Way requires all of the engaged couples who want to marry at the church or be married by pastors from the church to attend twelve two-hour premarital courses taught by an excellent team of teachers. These couples must also participate in three or four personal counseling sessions. They further take two personality tests and are required to read several books, including *If Only He Knew* by Gary Smalley (Zondervan) and *Creative Counterpart* by Linda Dillow (Thomas Nelson). Less than a month before the wedding they also read *Intended for Pleasure* by Ed and Gaye Wheat (Revell). Premarital counseling from Church on the Way makes for Christian couples on the way. It's small wonder that many couples who will ultimately marry at other churches come to get in on this counseling, too. Your church may not be able to provide such extensive preparation, but careful, biblical counseling is essential if you don't want to end up another unhappy statistic.

Considering elopement? The justice of the peace won't give you the kind of premarital counseling you need. Don't leave home without it!

Do Church Bells Have to Ring?

Sometimes I'm asked, "How important is a church wedding?" The answer is threefold:

First, a church wedding openly invites the anointing of God. The pastor performing the ceremony has usually held an important spiritual-teaching role in the life of at least one of the two getting married. His prayer, his leading the couple in the vows before Jesus Christ and his personal remarks can be a strong witness for Christ. One highlight during many wedding ceremonies is the moment the pastor speaks to the wedding guests and gives them the opportunity to receive Jesus Christ and be born again. "Wedding mills" where people are whisked in and out to legalize their marriages are cold and impersonal in comparison.

Second, the gathering of friends in itself is a wonderful way to launch a marriage. Their prayers and fellowship can be very meaningful. On a practical level, so can the gifts they bring.

Third, the memory of these things leaves a marker that later reminds both the bride and groom that they did tell the Lord they would stay married for a lifetime.

Strong Advice

If you are seriously thinking about marriage now or in the future, I urge you to read my book *Marriage Plus: The Bible and Marriage*, in which I carefully outline the role of both husband and wife, communication, sex, and so on. Remember: God invented marriage. It was His idea. If you really want to understand how something works, ask the inventor.

I recommend you also work through — together as a couple — Norm Wright's outstanding workbook of discussion questions, *Before You Say I Do* (Harvest House).

An Exciting Year

Engagement is a wonderful time of growth, learning, talking, listening and observing. How does he react when the soup falls in his lap, when he gets a flat tire, when he has a headache? How, and on what, does he spend his money? How polite is he? How does he talk about his parents? How does he act around her friends? How hard is he willing to work? How moral is he? Does he have a steady temperament, or does he blow up when things go wrong? How well does he take care of his body, both with cleanliness and with exercise? What are his hobbies, favorite sports, major interests, goals? How does he feel and behave around children and old people? Does he like to travel? What kind of music, television, movies does he enjoy? Does he read books and magazines? If so, what kind? Is he an early riser, a night owl? What are his favorite foods? Is he a complainer? Does he keep his word? Is he a sharp dresser? Does he swear? How artistic is he? Is he healthy? All these things need to be known about her too. And much more about both of them. Can you see why this will take at least a year of discovery?

An engagement, as thrilling as it will be, must be a very realistic time to be certain no flaw in either of you will risk ruining your love, your children or your marriage. There's still time to turn back before the two of you begin a lifetime of commitment to each other.

A lady should keep any frog that tells her,
"Kiss me and I'll turn into a prince."
With the economy as it is,
princes aren't worth much today.
But a talking frog is worth millions!

Questions for Reflection and Discussion

1. Write an answer to the letter preceding chapter 9. What does she need to think about during the year prior to marriage?

2. What do you think is the major role of the pastor or qualified church leader in premarital counseling? What role should your parents and close Christian friends play in your decision to become engaged to someone? Discuss this.

3. How can a couple work to become best friends *before* marriage? Does it take work to become best friends, or does it happen naturally? Discuss this.

4. In many parts of the world matchmaking by parents continues today. The parents look for the best match spiritually, socially, financially and so forth that their son or daughter could have. Consider this method of choosing a spouse. What are the good aspects of it? What don't you like about it? Is our present American system of marrying for "love" a superior system? Why? Why not? Discuss this.

5. Engagement is usually the last step before marriage and as such is a very critical time for the couple. What is the purpose of an engagement period? How does the concept of engagement today differ from the concept of betrothal during Jesus' day? How are the two concepts similar? Is either system superior to the other? Why? Why not? Discuss this.

Dear Ray,

I went to your Singles Plus seminar. I'm sure I'd be pregnant now if I hadn't heard your talks. My boyfriend (and now I'm ashamed to say I was even going with him!) was doing all kinds of things to me. I was stupidly letting him use my body for his thrills. You know, if I hadn't heard you, I probably would have ended up hating sex. Now it's something I look forward to when I get married, but I'm keeping myself for the right man. I wish all my friends could hear you. I can't wait to read your *Singles Plus* book. I'll be sharing what you say with everyone I know.

Saved and Saving Myself for Marriage

*Happy is the man who
doesn't give in and do wrong
when he is tempted,
for afterwards he will get
as his reward the crown of life
that God has promised
those who love him.*

James 1:12, LB

TEN

HOW TO KEEP YOUR SEX DRIVE IN NEUTRAL

The stops, as well as the steps,
of a good man are ordered by the Lord.

S omeone wrote Ann Landers this tragic poem:

I met him.
I liked him.
I liked him.
I loved him.
I loved him.
I let him.
I lost him.

Then someone from Fort Worth, Texas, wrote her this beautiful poem about his own experience:

> I saw her.
> I liked her.
> I loved her.
> I wanted her.
> I asked her.
> She said no.
> I married her.
> After 60 years,
> I still love her.[1]

The Wrong Way to Get Rid of Guilt

When I was a freelance news reporter in the San Francisco area during the Vietnam War, I was sent to cover a riot. Two hundred college-age Americans were lying in front of napalm trucks, blocking them from entering a port. The police and the young people screamed at each other, each side assured of its stand. I interviewed many people. The surprise statement of the day came from a police chief. Angry and shouting into my microphone, he said, "This is the fault of the churches! They teach about sin. If these kids didn't believe in sin, they wouldn't be worried about napalm and what it does to humans. The churches ought to be closed down."

Many people today feel the same way about the Bible and its approach to sex, along with the church: "Close down the church. If the church didn't teach about sin, no one would be concerned about immorality, abortion and 'safe sex,' and no one would feel guilty. The churches ought to be closed down."

Yet God invented sex. It was His beautiful idea in the first place. No one supports sex in marriage more strongly than God Himself (1 Cor. 7:3-5). Though there are some in the church who condemn all sex, it is His wedding gift to every bride and groom.

The church doesn't need to be closed down. It does need to discover what God has said about sex. Then it needs to help the world recover from its moral collapse. Nationwide surveys, including those by *Redbook* magazine, indicate that by and large religious people (Christians) have the best sex lives. That's because they don't carry the guilt many others live with.

You see, the world does know illicit sex is wrong. In March 1989 the Rhode Island Supreme Court ruled that a single divorced parent could not allow her boyfriend to sleep overnight when the children were home. In an interview, the

Rhode Island judge stated, "The court must infer the situation is not conducive to the welfare of the children." So the single woman involved and her attorneys appealed their case to the United States Supreme Court. The Supreme Court let the Rhode Island court's decision stand without comment. A precedent has now been established.[2]

According to *Single Adult Ministries Journal*,[3] in October 1989 the Minnesota Supreme Court ruled that refusing to rent to an unmarried couple does not amount to illegal discrimination. The court said the landlord is protected by his First Amendment "freedom of religion" right and can act on his religious convictions. A Minnesota law prohibiting fornication also worked on the landlord's behalf.

In a recent major national survey of 210,000 married couples, 85 percent of wives and 74 percent of husbands said they had *never* been sexually unfaithful. Canadian responses were almost identical.

Christ, who forgives and cleanses all who confess their sin to Him (1 John 1:9), gives the power to live a moral, fulfilled life with sex or without it. He declares all sex outside marriage gross sin (Heb. 13:4) because it is without the lifetime commitment of marriage. He wants to keep everyone free from guilt and the emotional and physical trauma so common among those who will not listen to Him.

The apostle Paul, writing during days of heavy persecution of all Christians, went so far as to say, "But if anyone feels he ought to marry because he has trouble controlling his passions, it is all right, it is not a sin; let him marry" (1 Cor. 7:36, LB).

If Arlyne had given in to my sexual advances, I'm sure I would never have married her. There are those who say, "I don't want a virgin. I want someone who's had a little experience." But analyze what they are saying: "I want someone who has cheated on God and violated His orders about sex." The cost for marrying such a person could be that they will break your heart after marriage by violating God's orders again. Or they might be bound up with guilt and fear about sex and try to avoid it entirely. Or they might give you a venereal disease. Is that what you really want?

> Flee immorality. Every other sin that a man [person] commits is outside the body, but the immoral man sins against his own body. Or do you not know that your body is a temple of the Holy Spirit who is in you, whom you have from God, and that you are not your own? For you have been bought with a price: therefore glorify God in your body (1 Cor. 6:18-20).

How often have you heard someone say, "All sins are alike"? First Corinthians

6:18 disagrees. It tells us clearly there is *no other sin like sexual immorality*. Some singles who have had intercourse give this excuse: "We figured we were already sinning with each other's bodies, so we might as well go all the way and have intercourse."

But each step taken by an unmarried person toward sexual intercourse is a sin compounding the sin that has previously been committed. It is sin upon sin upon sin that leads to the final sin of intercourse. Each sin is "a sin against the sinner's body," weakening it, robbing it of the Holy Spirit's ability to stop the damning sin of intercourse from happening (Rev. 21:8; 22:15).

Jim Burns has written an outstanding book, *Handling Your Hormones: The "Straight Scoop" on Love and Sexuality* (Harvest House), that may be helpful to you.

The Greek word translated *flee* means "run from." Joseph took God literally, even when Potiphar's wife wanted to go to bed with him:

> "How...could I do this great evil, and sin against God?" ...Now it happened one day that he went into the house to do his work, and none of the men of the household was there inside. And she caught him by his garment, saying, "Lie with me!" And he left his garment in her hand and fled, and went outside (Gen. 39:9, 11-12).

Joseph *ran* rather than commit sexual immorality. As a result, "The Lord was with him; and whatever he did, the Lord made to prosper" (Gen. 39:23). Joseph knew sexual immorality was a direct sin against God.

Contrast Joseph with David — in the wrong place at the wrong time. In the spring, when kings normally went to battle, King David stayed home (2 Sam. 11:1).

> Now when evening came David arose from his bed and walked around on the roof of the king's house, and from the roof he saw a woman bathing; and the woman was very beautiful in appearance.... And David sent messengers and took her, and when she came to him, he lay with her (vv. 2,4).

All it took was "the lust of the eyes" (1 John 2:15-17). It seemed so simple — until later. What was the outcome of David's sin? Deception and murder (2 Sam. 11:14-15); the death of David's baby (2 Sam. 12:14). And Psalm 38 may be referring to a contracted venereal disease. (Few writings could more clearly describe someone suffering from the hideous agony of a venereal disease.)

The High Cost of Sexual Immorality

Both mothers and fathers ask me, "Do you think I'd be helping my daughter by having her fitted with a diaphragm? Then if she did get tempted, she wouldn't end up with a baby." The answer is an absolute no! The moment a single person uses any form of birth control, he or she is telling God, "I don't know whether I'm going to follow You or not." The devil will work overtime to see that they fall. If birth control devices were foolproof, unwanted pregnancies and venereal disease would not be at the epidemic crisis level they are. Relying on birth control methods is like relying on a "lucky" rabbit's foot. Both offer false security.

Meanwhile, God is often called a spoilsport, because He forbids all forms of sexual immorality. Hollywood, the smut magazines and others who want sex outside marriage often call Christianity "archaic" and "too rigid" for this enlightened age. But let's take a look at the whole picture. *Is* sexual immorality "fun"?

The individual — and the community — pay a high price for sexual immorality. Sixty percent of American babies are conceived out of wedlock. There is an abortion in America every twenty-one seconds. One rape is reported in America every ten minutes.

Syphilis is at its highest rate in twenty years, infecting ninety thousand new victims every year. When left untreated, all symptoms disappear within six months. Ten years later it rears up, causing blindness, heart disease, paralysis, brain damage, insanity or death, as well as severe birth defects or death for babies.

Chlamydia strikes up to ten million American women annually. Women who take birth control pills are two to three times more likely to contract the disease, causing itching, burning and vaginal discharge and often premature or stillborn births. The chlamydia is transferred to the woman's babies, who regularly develop pneumonia or severe eye infections.

Genital herpes (which causes genital sores) is a close relative to oral herpes (which causes cold sores and fever blisters), and both are incurable and highly contagious. In the United States an estimated fifty million people have oral herpes and twenty-six to thirty-one million have genital herpes. Genital or venereal herpes causes an embarrassing itching and intense pain in the genital area, a burning sensation when urinating or a vaginal discharge. It also causes painful, fluid-filled blisters or sores on the vagina, cervix, urethra or anal area in women, and on the penis or around the anus in men. All the symptoms of a bad case of the flu accompany the onset of the disease. Genital and anal blisters recur off and on from then on.

The mental problems that accompany genital herpes can be even worse than the itching and pain itself. Deep depression, an intense desire to get away from everyone and the feeling of being an outcast are part of what is often called the "leper" effect of genital herpes. The majority of babies die whose mothers have a recurring attack of herpes at the time of delivery. Of the babies who survive, half suffer blindness or brain damage.

Gonorrhea infects one million people each year, often causing infertility or impotence. The disease may also cause insanity, brain damage, blindness, paralysis, arthritis, heart disease and death. Victims may notice a whitish discharge from the penis or vagina three to seven days after intercourse with an infected person. But it is terribly deceptive. Four out of five women and one out of five men have no sign at all until the disease has done its damage.

Genital or venereal warts affect one million new victims each year. All types of the disease are linked to cervical cancer. When babies inherit these warts, they get them in their throats and lungs.

Then there's AIDS (Acquired Immune Deficiency Syndrome). "The number of people who test positive for the AIDS virus is now doubling every sixteen months. By far the largest percent of these victims are homosexual men and drug abusers. But a 1985-1989 study of more than one million teenage recruits to the military revealed HIV infection (the AIDS virus) is equally distributed between men and women."[4]

Full-blown AIDS destroys the body's ability to ward off infections, killing 80 percent of its victims within a few years. Symptoms in children include nerve damage and respiratory problems. There is no known cure for this disease.

The medical science community is shaken. Most of the diseases listed above — in fact, all thirty-nine sexually transmitted diseases now spreading — are immune to antibiotics. Penicillin isn't getting the job done. "Free sex" carries an extremely high price tag.

When you have sex, you are exposing yourself to any sexual disease carried by anyone your partner has had sex with in the past ten years. Anyone who has had any immoral sexual contact within the past ten years should get an AIDS test immediately. In fact, genital or venereal warts can be infectious as long as a carrier is sexually active. If you've *ever* been immoral, you need an STD test.

So *is* sex outside marriage "fun"?

The Truth About Condoms

Some have asked, "Why shouldn't I use a condom or birth control? I won't have a baby then."

First, God condemns the act of marriage outside marriage. He grants no special indulgences because you are using mechanical devices during the act. Second, the risk of pregnancy or venereal disease can't be overstated. There is only one 100 percent foolproof birth control method. It's called abstinence!

All birth control devices have serious disadvantages; nearly all can create some measure of physical damage in women.

Do condoms offer "safe sex"? *U.S. News and World Report* magazine gave an honest report on condoms in October 1987. Here are just some of the facts:

Sexual restraint, says an AIDS handbook for schools issued last week by the Department of Education, is the "safest" and smartest way to prevent infection. Condoms, on the other hand, "can reduce, but not eliminate the risk." No one *can* say how much protection the condoms offer....

Condoms are made of latex or animal membrane. Packages are clearly labeled. Membrane condoms, which are several times more expensive, are much riskier. Some studies indicate viral particles can pass through them. But...with a failure rate of 10 to 15 percent, latex condoms aren't a perfect form of birth control. And to keep AIDS from spreading, a condom must work ten times better. A woman is fertile roughly 36 days a year, but someone with AIDS can transmit 365 days a year.

...Dr. Michael Rosenberg of the American Social Health Association, a group that tracks sexually transmitted diseases, estimates that condoms may reduce the chances of getting AIDS by about half. That's about the protection they afford for other sexually transmitted diseases. But no one has good numbers, since some condoms burst and others are removed too soon or otherwise used incorrectly.

...Anecdotal reports suggest that anal sex, a common practice among gays and a small portion of heterosexuals, damages condoms.

...Many experts say definitive data may *never* be available, because it is unethical to set up a study in which one group has unprotected sex with infected partners while another group uses condoms.[5]

Remember: condoms "have a failure rate of 10 to 15 percent" and cut the possibility of getting a venereal disease only by "about half." So any time one is used it is simply a matter of Russian roulette with even more bullets in the chamber! Is it any surprise so many babies are created this way and so much venereal disease continues to spread?

God's Love and Venereal Disease

Christ came to bring each of us abundant life. But Satan "comes only to steal, and kill, and destroy" (John 10:10). Venereal disease is part of the destruction kit the devil uses on those who rebel against God. In Exodus 15:26 God told His people,

> If you will give earnest heed to the voice of the Lord your God, and do what is right in His sight, and give ear to His commandments, and keep all His statutes, I will put none of the diseases on you which I have put on the Egyptians; for I, the Lord, am your healer.

The devil is "powerless" against God (Heb. 2:14). But those who yield to the devil unwittingly or willingly welcome disease.

Would a loving God allow venereal disease? Writing about homosexuality and lesbianism, Paul said,

> For this reason God gave them over to degrading passions; for their women exchanged the natural function for that which is unnatural, and in the same way also the men abandoned the natural function of the woman and burned in their desire toward one another, men with men committing indecent acts and receiving in their own persons the due penalty of their error (Rom. 1:26-27).

Every homosexual encounter is gross sin and always gambles hideous disease, life itself and the destruction of the homosexual's nation. As Jude 7 (LB) warns, "And don't forget the cities of Sodom and Gomorrah and their neighboring towns, all full of lust of every kind including lust of men for other men. Those cities were destroyed by fire and continue to be a warning to us that there is a hell in which sinners are punished."

Yet a perverted sexual encounter or a season of such sin does not mean the one involved is a homosexual or lesbian. Most who have fallen into this perversion realize they do not want to continue in such a life-style and break free from it.

Adulterers and fornicators are equally guilty in His sight. Jesus Christ offers every sexually immoral person His power to break free (John 8:36).

Other Regrets

Venereal disease may be the most obvious regret of immorality, but it's not the only one. Serious sexual studies nationwide make four important points about sexual relations outside marriage.

1. There's no full security for anyone outside marriage. So the very act of sex is extremely different from how it would be within the security of marriage. Most normal females require security to relax and enjoy foreplay and the act of sex. For

them, sex can't be fully enjoyed outside marriage.

2. Some people enjoy sex only when it's immoral. Once they're married, it loses its thrill. Often you can't tell who such people are until they're married. Then it's too late.

3. Living together without marriage becomes heartbreak for most couples in less than two years.

4. No matter how good it looks, you can't violate God's rules without hell to pay (Rev. 21:8; 22:15).

What Is Sexual Sin?

For the unmarried God forbids far more than intercourse. He also forbids what is commonly called foreplay, which is a God-ordained, God-blessed passion when used as designed — in marriage. Why? Because God "does not tempt anyone" (James 1:13). God works to keep His people away from all temptation. All of the following actions are forbidden by the Lord:

Fornication — illicit sexual relations involving an unmarried person with someone else. It usually refers to sexual intercourse between them. Fornication is forbidden in Acts 15:19-20; 1 Corinthians 7:2; Hebrews 13:4.

Adultery — illicit sexual relations involving a married person with someone else. It usually refers to sexual intercourse between them. Adultery is forbidden in Matthew 15:18-20, Hebrews 13:4 and Revelation 2:20-22.

Concupiscence — an unchecked immoral drive that wants what it wants when it wants it. Concupiscence is forbidden in Romans 7:8, Colossians 3:4-5 and 1 Thessalonians 4:3-5.

Lasciviousness (also called *sensuality* or *licentiousness*) — the act of making up moral rules that violate God's moral rules. Lasciviousness is forbidden in Galatians 5:19-21, Ephesians 4:17-24 and Jude 4.

Defrauding — arousing sexual appetites in someone else that cannot be righteously fulfilled because doing so would violate God's moral rules. Defrauding is forbidden in Mark 10:19, 1 Thessalonians 4:2-8 and James 1:14-15.

Why These Rules?

As Larry Tomczak explains:

> Jesus gives us moral laws not to undercut our enjoyment of life and frustrate us like muzzled hounds at a barbecue, but He gives them because He loves us and desires to discipline us in a way that will best bring us into the fullness of all life has to offer. The key is knowing the

169

Person behind these laws — that He loves us and demonstrated it on Calvary. Otherwise they appear as just some legalistic code.

In the area of sex, God has put limitations on the display of affection prior to marriage because He wants us to experience a *maximum* marriage with a *maximum* sex life. (This I now speak from experience!)[6]

Fornication and adultery break God's heart (1 Cor. 6:18-20). These sins cause the sinner the instant loss of his or her testimony for Christ. They also break the sinner's heart, either now or in the future. There is no way to get virginity back once it has been lost. What will you give your spouse on your wedding night that has not already been given away to someone else?

If you are reading this and have already lost your virginity, please know that Jesus Christ not only forgives but "cleanses from *all* unrighteousness" (1 John 1:9, italics added). For those who honestly repent and abandon their sin, "cleanse" means Christ restores the "cleansed" as if they had *never* sinned. Stay clean and no matter how long you were immoral, you will enter your marriage as if you had never committed sexual sin. This is not license to continue in sin. "Go, and sin no more" (John 8:11b).

In *Youth Aflame* Winkie Pratney writes:

> The boy who thinks sex sin "does no harm, as long as you don't hurt anyone" is a fool. The chief pleasure of "sexual conquest" for a male is not physical, but primarily psychological...the thrill of "putting it over!" Such a conquest not only degrades God's purpose but enslaves him to lust, sows the seed of distrust in his partner of any future marriage, and can never really satisfy. It can never achieve the heights of a real love relationship such as that God planned for man and wife — one of mutual trust and confidence.
>
> Likewise the girl who gives her body to a boy "in love" with her, expects to be rewarded with understanding and affection, but will always be disappointed. Without God-ordained sanctions, there can be no mutual giving and tender affection, no leisure to develop a warm relationship and a guilt-free happiness together.[7]

How Far Is Too Far?

If you were double-dating with another couple, and suddenly they went into a passionate kissing session that lasted for several minutes, would it mean anything to you? It should. If it didn't, it might be strong evidence your conscience has been seared with a hot iron (1 Tim. 4:2). The conscience's warning alarm is seldom turned off abruptly. It is turned off a degree at a time. Many people who consider themselves good Christians have allowed their own consciences to be numbed by today's mass media magic.

Every kiss should mean something. When a kiss becomes casual it has no meaning. It falls far short of "an expression of love." Anyone who hands out kisses like candy will have to do something more to put real meaning in romantic involvement. This quickly gets spiritually dangerous. What can that "more" be that doesn't violate God's orders?

French kissing, one's tongue probing into the other's mouth, is sexually arousing. Anyone who isn't defrauded by French kissing either dislikes the experience or has almost no sex drive. "Then when lust has conceived, it gives birth to sin; and when sin is accomplished, it brings forth death" (James 1:15) — spiritual death as one surrenders to the forbidden; emotional death as one allows his or her conscience to be numbed; and physical death, which often starts with guilt, fear and bitterness when the violated person realizes he or she has been used. If intercourse follows, a baby could die, too, through abortion or disease.

You may read the above paragraph and say, "That's ridiculous. Intercourse doesn't necessarily follow French kissing." Technically that's true. But when one begins the act of defrauding, one can quickly find reason for lasciviousness.

The step that usually follows French kissing is petting, where hands touch the other person's private parts. It includes everything from touching her clothed or unclothed breasts to mutual masturbation. Singles often ask me, "Why can't we pet? After all, we're going to be married." But you have no guarantee of that. Besides, God forbids sex even one half-second before marriage (1 Cor. 7:2). God is not mean. You would be staggered by the number of women who tell me, "I don't like sex. My husband and I are married. God says our sex life is pure. But we violated God before we married, and every time my husband touches me now, it's just like when we weren't married. I hate sex because of what we did then."

Petting is a prelude to intercourse because it stimulates the one being petted and makes him or her want to go all the way. It defrauds and cannot be entered into without lasciviousness. It continually feeds concupiscence.

Someone may say, "My girlfriend or boyfriend and I are petting, and it hasn't led to sexual intercourse." My answer is, it hasn't yet. But even if it never does, you are breaking God's moral laws. You can't touch fire without getting burned (Prov. 6:27).

The Law of Diminishing Returns

If you are involved with someone and are going beyond the good-night kiss, you are already discovering the law of diminishing returns. Each new step into forbidden territory becomes another step closer to intercourse. It is very hard to stop what you've been doing, but stopping can be done by two Christians who believe God's Word and want to obey it (John 14:15). Christ has magnificent blessings for those who make their bodies "living sacrifices" so they can discover "the perfect will of God" for their lives (Rom. 12:1-2).

What About Masturbation?

> Do you not know that your body is a temple of the Holy Spirit who is in you, whom you have from God, and that you are not your own? For you have been bought with a price: therefore glorify God in your body (1 Cor. 6:19-20).

As a Christian your body is never your own. While you are unmarried, your body is owned by God. When married, your body belongs to your spouse (1 Cor. 7:4) and God (1 Cor. 6:19-20).

The Bible does not directly mention anything about masturbation. Rest assured, masturbation won't make hair grow on your palms. Nor will it cause you to go blind. Matthew 5:30 — "If your right hand makes you stumble, cut it off" — does not refer to masturbation. Statistics show the vast majority of both males and females, from puberty on, do try masturbation.

Genesis 38:9 — "Onan...wasted his seed on the ground..." — has nothing to do with masturbation, but with coitus interruptus. The man withdrew from his dead brother's wife after beginning to have intercourse with her and ejaculated on the ground. There is nothing wrong with this act in marriage, but Onan was directly disobeying God in this case. Under God's orders he was supposed to give his dead brother an heir. (By the way, this is a terrible form of birth control because a male doesn't have to ejaculate in order to produce a baby; he can simply leave a trace of sperm in the female. Some men do this without knowing it because they do not feel anything when it happens.)

In the King James version of 1 Corinthians 6:9-10 Paul condemns "abusers of themselves" as those who will "not inherit the kingdom of God." Some have mistakenly thought this term referred to those who masturbate. But all later Bible translations such as the New American Standard and the New International Version correctly translate "abusers of themselves" from the original Greek language as "homosexuals."

Because of the Bible's silence regarding masturbation, some outstanding Christian teachers have endorsed a limited practice of masturbation for the purpose of self-control. Many other outstanding Christian teachers take a hard line against any masturbation.

After counseling thousands of married couples and singles, I have noted three major recurring problems that accompany masturbation:

1. *Sexual fantasies.* Matthew 5:27-28, James 1:14-15 and 1 John 2:15-17 strongly forbid giving yourself to *any* sexual fantasies.

Someone once said, "The world says you're free in sex through indulgence. God says you're free in sex through control. Until you can control this area of your life as a single person, you're not free. You're in bondage to your passions."

The more you allow your mind to dwell on anything you'd really like to do, the more apt you are to do it.

2. *Singles who masturbate often find it hard to stop once they are married.* When masturbation continues after marriage, serious marital problems usually result. The spouse feels cheated and abandoned.

3. *Masturbation can become a fleshly bondage that drives a person into loneliness and shame.* While they do not refer directly to masturbation, two verses underline this truth: "But we have renounced the things hidden because of shame" (2 Cor. 4:2). Few people of moral character would masturbate with anyone else present. It is a "hidden thing," precisely because it is an act that brings shame. Most Christians who masturbate feel ashamed about it.

> For this is the will of God, your sanctification; that is, that you abstain from sexual immorality; that each of you know how to possess his own vessel in sanctification and honor, not in lustful passion, like the Gentiles who do not know God (vv. 3-5).

Possessing one's "own vessel in sanctification and honor, not in lustful passion" is difficult for most people who regularly masturbate. The person who engages in this activity often feels dirty, not sanctified or Christ-centered. It becomes an act of self-gratification with the terrible price of a loss of self-respect.

Masturbation is not a damning sin. But it often undermines a Christian's close walk with Christ. Anything that risks doing *that* is not worth doing.

For an excellent message on this subject, send for Jack Hayford's teaching "Solo Sex: Release or Rejection?"[8]

Temptation Isn't Sin

Someone has said, "There are two dogs inside every Christian — the old dog [your old life] and the new dog [your Christian life]. The dog that wins is the one you feed."

Lust and *temptation* are not synonymous. *Temptation* is a thought that may or may not give in to lust. *Lust* is a continual commitment of the mind to do something if you could. Temptation is not sin. Jesus Christ was "tempted in all things as we are, yet without sin" (Heb. 4:15).

Jesus Christ knows exactly how to help you beat the devil's game. He knew and used God's Word, just as you and I can. He quoted the Bible and shut the devil's mouth (Matt. 4).

You will never be tempted beyond your ability to resist. God will always give you "the way of escape" from it (1 Cor. 10:13). That way isn't given when you're entangled with someone on a mattress. It is given long before that, for example, when you could turn down a date with someone whose morals you question. Charles Spurgeon said, "Learn to say no. It will be of more use to you than to be able to read Latin." Temptation will definitely knock on your door, but it's your fault if you invite it in for the evening.

A Short Course in Beating Sexual Temptation

The truth is that, although of course we lead normal human lives, the battle we are fighting is on the spiritual level. The very weapons we use are not those of human warfare but powerful in God's warfare for the destruction of the enemy's strongholds. Our battle is to bring down every deceptive fantasy and every imposing defense that men erect against the true knowledge of God. We even fight to capture every thought until it acknowledges the authority of Christ (2 Cor. 10:3-5, Phillips).

1. *Hate sin.* Any real victory over the devil will only be won if you want to win it. Sin put Jesus Christ on the cross. You can't really love Jesus Christ unless you hate sin. Those who overcome sin have a biblical "perfect hatred" against sin (Ps. 139:22).

2. *Identify when and where your temptation usually occurs.* Are you alone or with others when you feel it? What situation triggers it? Ask the Lord to show you how to change this situation. Do what He says. You may need to change friends too. "He who walks with wise men will be wise, but the companion of fools will be destroyed" (Prov. 13:20, NKJV).

3. *Don't help the tempter.* Satan is "the tempter" (Matt. 4:3; 1 Thess. 3:5). He needs no help from you. The things that most turn a guy on physically are how he is touched and what he sees. If a woman touches him anywhere near his genital area, she will tempt him — or defraud him. If she wears a low-cut blouse, short skirt, tight sweater or the like, he will have a hard time resisting temptation. On the other hand, she will be tempted by a male's touch and the romantic words he

174

speaks. If he touches her anywhere near her breasts or genital area, he will tempt her. If he speaks sensual words to her, she may also be tempted. Neither the male nor the female should be touched on the legs above the knees.

4. *Believe you can change.* You can do anything Christ gives you the strength to do (Phil. 4:13). Honestly ask Him for the strength not to give in.

5. *Run!* If things get out of hand, follow Joseph's example and flee! Grab the handle of the car door or the apartment and leave. You can phone later and explain your actions briefly.

I recommend that every woman keep a stun gun in her purse. A stun gun is an electrically charged, battery-operated gun about the size of a woman's compact. It gives off a stunning jolt that will paralyze a person for several minutes but will cause no permanent harm when used correctly. One woman told me she had a date who tried to rape her. When things got out of her control, she said, "Wait, let me get you a condom." She reached in her purse, pulled out her stun gun and zapped him! Then she ran and got away.

A Longer Course in Running From Temptation

What you see, read and take in through your eyes will greatly determine the quality of your sexual fulfillment. You've got to be especially careful about swallowing lies. A commercial rightly warns, "The mind is a terrible thing to waste." The devil works overtime to waste your mind.

Let's look at a few of his old tricks heightened in potency by the mass media and modern technology.

We live in a day when sexual temptation sells everything from jeans to perfume. Technicolor sexual fantasies provide sights and sounds more tantalizing than many a heathen king enjoyed as he watched his harem dancers. Madison Avenue can get Americans to buy almost anything. Good advertising has a motto: "Sell the sizzle, not the steak."

But the smut merchants aren't limited to advertising. In his challenging newsletter *Media Update*, Al Menconi asked, "Is TV Destroying Christianity?" What he says of TV is also true of movies.

> What would be your opinion of a man who spends his evenings prowling through neighborhoods peeking into bedroom windows and watching couples having sex? He roams from neighborhood to neighborhood looking for new experiences to satisfy his sexual appetite.... Would you consider a person who spends his evenings and some daytime hours viewing the sexual practices of people in your neighborhood a pervert? I would.

Isn't *that* what television is doing to us when it takes our mind's eye into bedroom after bedroom, night after night, channel after channel? How many times do we sit and watch immoral scenes and programs and justify it by saying the immorality is only secondary to the whole story?

...Any man who says that he can watch a steamy sexual encounter and not be encouraged to lust has a much more serious problem that we don't have time to discuss. These shows *do* encourage lust. Lust is stimulating.... The Bible clearly states that we are to "take every thought captive to the obedience of Christ" (2 Cor. 10:5) and "flee our lusts" (2 Tim. 2:22), not stimulate them.[9]

In July 1987, when Duke University awarded newsman Ted Koppel an honorary doctor of humane letters degree, Koppel focused his address on the Ten Commandments. Relating them to the television industry, he said:

In the place of *truth*, we have discovered *facts*. For moral absolutes, we have substituted moral ambiguity. We now communicate with everyone and say absolutely nothing. We have reconstructed the Tower of Babel, and it is a television antenna.... We are beginning to make our mark on the American people. We have actually convinced ourselves that slogans will save us. Shoot up, if you must, but use a clean needle. Enjoy sex whenever and with whomever you wish, but wear a condom.

"No." The answer is "no." Not because it isn't cool or smart or because you might end up in jail or dying in an AIDS ward, but "no" because it's *wrong*.... I caution you, as one who performs daily on that flickering altar [of television], to set your sights beyond what you can see....[10]

Writing to the church at Philippi, Paul wrote:

Finally, brethren, whatever is true, whatever is honorable, whatever is right, whatever is pure, whatever is lovely, whatever is of good repute, if there is any excellence and if anything worthy of praise, let your mind dwell on these things. The things you have learned and received and heard and seen in me, practice these things; and the God of peace shall be with you (Phil. 4:8-9).

How much peace do you have? "Don't let the world around you squeeze you into its mold" (Rom. 12:2, Phillips). Conscience doesn't get its guidance from a

Gallup Poll or a movie critic. Foul up your conscience, and it may never speak nicely to you again.

A New TV Guide

At least twenty years ago I found a list of questions called "Your TV Guide" at a church. Which church? Who wrote them? I have no idea. But this list has served me faithfully as both a television and movie guide. I have added to the list as I've thought about more problems that often arise when watching programs or films. You may want to add to it too.

Before a program or movie, ask yourself these questions:
1. Why am I considering watching this program or going to this movie?
2. What has this program been like in the past, or what have I heard or read in the advertisements about this film?
3. Is this a good way to be informed or entertained?
4. Would watching this program or movie with anyone else risk harm to that person? If so, why would *I* not risk harm by seeing it?
5. Are alcohol and other drugs glamorized or taken for granted?
6. Does this program or movie honestly represent Jesus Christ, the Bible and Christianity? Does it follow biblical principles or make fun of them? If I see anything that mocks God, shouldn't I turn the dial or walk out of the film and ask for my money back?

After a program or movie:
1. Am I a better person for having watched it?
2. Was I encouraged in morality or immorality?
3. Should I consider seeing it again or ever recommending it? Why?
4. How can I use what I have learned to honor God?
5. Should I communicate my convictions about this program to advertisers or television stations and networks?

If you do walk out of a movie, with or without a date, ask for your money back. Be polite in your attitude, but tell the manager you can't watch the film because of its contents. Give your reasons why. If enough Christians do this, movie managers will think much harder about the kinds of films they book in the future. If you walk out and don't ask for your money back, the manager has made a profit on you and has no hint of your objections.

If you disapprove of a television film or program because of objectionable material, let the sponsors know and also write both the local station and the

177

network. Christians are losing their moral and legal rights because they don't write. Advertisers pay attention to a polite letter stating objections, and so do the stations and networks. When it applies, tell advertisers you will not buy their products until they stop sponsoring objectionable programs. Then keep your word. Immediate phone calls also make an impression.

The Power of Music

I really look forward to hearing King David play his harp in heaven. Saul's demon didn't have a chance when David played that thing (1 Sam. 16:23). But today certain forms of music seem to invite demons rather than drive them out. If you listen to the devil pipe suggestions into your mind through song lyrics, you're going to be short-circuiting your walk with Christ. That would be true whether those lyrics were from rock music, country Western or any other kind of music.

In their book *Today's Music: A Window to Your Child's Soul*, Al Menconi and Dave Hart write,

> The Bible didn't say that if you listen to satanic music, you become a satanist. The Bible didn't say if you listen to sexually perverted music, you become a sexual pervert. The Bible didn't say that if you listen to rebellious music, you become rebellious. The Bible says that if you choose to entertain yourself with philosophies that are against biblical values, you will struggle with your faith in Jesus Christ (Col. 2:8).[11]

The Problem With Pornography

Pornography is an $8 billion-plus industry (annually) in America. Hiding behind the First Amendment, it degrades women; it has obvious links to rape, incest and child abuse; it dirties sex; and it robs millions of people from finding the fulfillment God planned sex to bring in marriage. Do you stay away from pornography?

Pornography "worship[s] and serve[s] the creature rather than the Creator" (Rom. 1:25), and pornography lies. Women do not have perfect bodies. Books, magazines and films distort the truth about sex and feed the reader's mind with false information about how much women like to be slapped and handled roughly, how heroes always have sex with several women, how much women love anal sex and so forth. One distortion leads to another, and the consumer is left with an "education" that is far worse than no sex education at all.

Charles Colson, former special counsel to President Nixon and founder of Prison Fellowship, wrote the following in "Celebrity Corner" for *USA Today*:

In his celebrated interview the night before his execution, mass murderer Ted Bundy told psychologist Dr. James Dobson how his obsession with hard-core pornography eventually led to his acting out the material he consumed. Murder fused his fascinations with twisted sex and violent death....

The demand for pornography, like the demand for drugs, is an addiction that feeds on the notion that there is no value above immediate gratification. It is fueled by the prevailing attitude that one must "grab all the gusto you can get." The only controlling factor is how one defines gusto....[12]

Ted Bundy described the desensitizing that caused him to change from nice guy to serial killer. He began with soft-core pornography. As many do with drugs, he soon craved something stronger. He said his moral progression went from tender love to rough love to rape to murder acted out in hard-core pornographic detail (as portrayed in the books and films he devoured).

In Josh McDowell's book *Givers, Takers, and Other Kinds of Lovers*, Gerhardt Dirks, one of the men who invented the computer, told McDowell what programs the male mind:

A lot of men and women are very casual about what they see or how they are touched. As a result, they numb the very sensorial areas God created to arouse and fulfill them sexually. To express his attitude of freedom and liberation, a guy may surround himself with pin-ups and lots of visual stimuli. He may frequent sexually stimulating movies. The long-term result will be a loss of sensitivity to the very things which God designed to fulfill him within the security of the marriage relationship. Because of this loss, it will constantly take more and more intense sexual stimulation to produce the same degree of arousal.[13]

My wife, Arlyne, tells me the secret of a clean desk is a large wastebasket. That is also the secret of a clean mind. Get rid of the junk in your mind. Turn off whatever television programs you shouldn't be watching. Stop going to movies that could damage your mind. (If you are at a movie, go out and buy popcorn while the previews of coming films are shown. Don't leave a date sitting in the theater either. Some of the worst scenes are in the previews.) Keep away from music, magazines and books that can devour you. Let Jesus Christ transform your mind instead.

Let me say this, then, speaking for the Lord: Live no longer as the unsaved do, for they are blinded and confused. Their closed hearts are full of darkness; they are far away from the life of God because they have shut their minds against him, and they cannot understand his ways. They don't care anymore about right and wrong and have given themselves over to impure ways. They stop at nothing, being driven by their evil minds and reckless lusts.

But that isn't the way Christ taught you! If you have really heard his voice and learned from him the truths concerning himself, then throw off your old evil nature....

Now your attitudes and thoughts must all be constantly changing for the better. Yes, you must be a new and different person, holy and good. Clothe yourself with this new nature (Eph. 4:17-24, LB).

How to Avoid Fouling Out

Wilt Chamberlain is my kind of basketball player. In his entire career he never had to leave a single game because of personal fouls. In the game of life Paul said there are two things you need to keep from fouling out:

This command I entrust to you, Timothy, my son, in accordance with the prophecies previously made concerning you, that by them you may fight the good fight, keeping faith and a good conscience, which some have rejected and suffered shipwreck in regard to their faith (1 Tim. 1:18-19).

Paul says some who originally had the faith fouled out and shipwrecked. Why? (1) They didn't keep the faith. (2) They didn't keep a clean conscience. Ignoring your conscience is like giving sleeping pills to your watchdog. How strong is your faith in Christ? How's your conscience? Keep both shipshape, and you won't be shipwrecked.

Though Satan is "the god of this world" (2 Cor. 4:4), Christ has given His believers full authority over the devil. When He died on the cross, Jesus Christ rendered the devil powerless against His believers (Heb. 2:14). In Matthew 28:18 Christ told us, "All authority has been given to Me in heaven and on earth." His very next words were, "Go therefore..." (v. 19). As long as we are surrendered to Jesus Christ as our Lord, we can "go therefore" using Christ's power to stop the devil's power. "Greater is He who is in [the Christian] than he who is in the world" (1 John 4:4).

What If You Do Foul Out?

If you fail at any point, ask for forgiveness (1 John 1:9). But make no excuses for yourself. God knows your heart — whether or not you're sincere in praying for His help to avoid temptation or to quit a bad habit. If you are, He will move heaven and earth to help you. If you aren't, praying to Him wouldn't accomplish anything (Matt. 15:7-8). "For godly sorrow produces repentance leading to salvation, not to be regretted; but the sorrow of the world produces death" (2 Cor. 7:10, NKJV).

Godly sorrow grieves over any breach in the relationship with Christ caused by sin. It demands a total breaking with the sin in every way (1 Thess. 5:22). The sorrow of the world regrets whatever consequences the sin brings into the sinner's life. This kind of sorrow will return to the sin if it gets the chance. But, as Jesus asked, "Why do you call Me, 'Lord, Lord,' and do not do what I say?" (Luke 6:46).

The Terrible Consequences of Sin

Sin looks so attractive when it tempts. But sin deceives (Heb. 3:13). It's like seeing a mirage on a desert; you think you have found something wonderful, until you find it doesn't fulfill your need at all. Don't give in to anything that will destroy your peace, your health, your life or your possible future marriage.

Christ's protection of the woman caught in the very act of adultery is a beautiful example of His love for everyone. His final words to her were, "Neither do I condemn you; go your way. From now on sin no more" (John 8:11). But this episode brings up some heavy questions. After Christ saved her from the self-righteous Pharisees, that woman still had to go home and face the music: What did the Pharisees say and do afterward? Do you really believe their wagging tongues were stopped regarding her? What did her family say and do? What did they think when they found out what she had done? How did it affect the rest of their lives? Did this woman repent and never commit this sin again? Christ had already warned about the risk people face who *do* sin again after they have been forgiven by Him. After healing the paralytic man, He told him, "Do not sin anymore, so that nothing worse may befall you" (John 5:14).

God's Promises for Those Who Win Over Temptation

If you keep My commandments, you will abide in My love; just as I have kept My Father's commandments, and abide in His love (John 15:10).

Blessed is a man [person] who perseveres under trial; for once he has been approved, he will receive the crown of life, which the Lord has promised to those who love Him (James 1:12).

There is laid up for me the crown of righteousness, which the Lord, the righteous Judge, will award to me on that day; and not only to me, but also to all who have loved His appearing (2 Timothy 4:8).

If you love Me, you will keep My commandments (John 14:15).

A Temporal Reward

Let me quote again from Josh McDowell's *Givers, Takers, and Other Kinds of Lovers*. In this passage Gerhardt Dirks expands on the positive benefits of the mind's ability to be programmed sexually.

If a man's initial programming is with his wife, and hers with her husband, the first lovemaking encounter provides an initial burst of data and pleasure response in both of them. Those patterns of initiation and response are filed away in their minds. Their next sexual encounter adds to it and expands it further. And the hundreds of subsequent experiences of life, interaction, and the physical sharing of love continue to build and further refine their mental programs.

It's not hard to understand, then, why sex within marriage doesn't become boring, but rather more satisfying over an entire lifetime. When properly programmed, our minds are an incredible organ for sexual fulfillment.[14]

When a person doesn't heed the above advice and instead has multiple sexual experiences with others, he or she is left in a land of comparison. After marriage the person is often not satisfied because "someone else did it better." Divorce often follows dissatisfaction.

Arlyne and I didn't have a great sex life when we began our marriage. It took patient time to develop. Wow, was it worth it! Take it from one who knows — marital sex is worth waiting for.

God's blessings or God's curses:
it's up to you.

Questions for Reflection and Discussion

1. Giving in to temptation is the first step in being mastered by the enemy. Carefully study James 1:13-15. Temptation does NOT come from God. What steps does James 4:7-10 tell you to take when you are faced with temptation? How can you know when you are being tempted? Can people ultimately overcome temptation without the help of the Lord? After writing down the steps for resisting temptation, discuss these issues.

2. First Corinthians 6:18 warns, "Flee immorality. Every other sin that a [person] commits is outside the body, but the immoral [person] sins against [his or her] own body." This verse makes it clear that when it comes to sexual sin, there are consequences against our bodies, the "temple of the Holy Spirit" (1 Cor. 6:19). Besides venereal disease and the risk of pregnancy outside wedlock, what are the consequences it brings to Christ's church ("the body of Christ," Eph. 4:12)? Why do you think sexual sins are so common today even among those who call themselves Christians? Are Christians in any way exempt from the consequences of sexual sins? Why does the Lord discipline His sons and daughters when they sin? Read Hebrews 12:5-13 to formulate your answer.

3. Second Timothy 2:22 in the Living Bible warns, "Run from anything that gives you the evil thoughts that young men often have, but stay close to anything that makes you want to do right. Have faith and love, and enjoy the companionship of those who love the Lord and have pure hearts." Have there been times in the past six months when you have been besieged with "evil thoughts"? Have any of your "friends," male or female, purposely contributed to your "evil thoughts"? If so, what should you do about your relationship with them? Read James 1:14-15. What will happen when you don't deal promptly with evil thoughts? Discuss this.

4. Carefully read 1 Corinthians 6:18; 1 Timothy 6:12-14; 2 Timothy 2:3-5,22; and 1 John 2:15-17. What do these verses have in common? Now think about the television programs, movies, books, magazines, music and so on to which you have given your eyes or ears during the last year. What impact have they had on you for better or for worse? In light of these verses, why do Christians have to be so careful to screen what they see and hear? Do single Christians have to be more careful than married Christians to screen what they see and hear? Why or why not? Discuss this.

5. Look again at the five terms used in this chapter to describe different types of sexual sin: fornication, adultery, concupiscence, lasciviousness and defrauding. Carefully read each verse cited as a reference for each term. People often wonder what constitutes sexual sin. How can a thorough understanding of these verses and terms help you in your relationship with people you date? Can you violate any of them without going too far? Discuss your answers.

Dear Ray,

   I am forty years old today. But this is not a happy birthday. I know you teach Marriage Plus and Singles Plus seminars. Well, when am I going to get a Marriage Plus for my singleness? I want to get married. I am beginning to panic, because I don't see anything that remotely looks like a possibility. I am thinking today, What if I never get married? I don't like that thought. Is there life after forty if I never get married? Tell me, please.

Unhappy Birthday to Me!

*And we know that God
causes all things to work together
for good to those who love God,
to those who are called
according to His purpose.*

Romans 8:28

ELEVEN

WHAT IF I NEVER GET MARRIED?

God will mend a broken heart,
if you will give Him all the pieces.

M aybe you once had a wonderful marriage. Widowed, you now live with memories. Or you may have loved some man or woman who took you to the heights of romantic love, then walked out and left you. You ache from loneliness. You may be single and never married. You may wish someone would tell you he or she wants to be with you forever. Maybe you've prayed and prayed and prayed, and yet you remain alone. There are times when it seems God doesn't really care.

To some Christians, the words of Jesus Christ in John 14:14 seem to mock those who've waited a long time without receiving an answer from God: "If you ask Me anything in My name, I will do it" (John 14:14). Likewise Matthew records, "For everyone who asks receives" (Matt. 7:8).

What does it take to get a miracle? A problem. In fact, the greater the problem, the greater the miracle! It's not really the problem that matters — it's what you do with it. You need to hang on and believe God for your miracle no matter how long you've waited. Luke 18:1 tells you to "pray and not to lose heart." You are not to quit on God while you wait. Expect a miracle!

God's promise to you is that as you seek to follow Him, staying within His Word and praying, He will (1) give you what you wish (John 15:7) *or* (2) do "beyond all that [you] ask or think" (Eph. 3:20). That's not a tricky way to sweep all unanswered prayers under the carpet. That's the truth. The question you need to settle is this: Would you rather have the best *you* can imagine or the best *He* can imagine for you? The honest answer to that question shows how much you trust Jesus Christ as Lord of your life.

To the single who has been abandoned, "Sing...for your Creator will be your 'husband.' ...For the Lord has called you back from your grief — a young wife abandoned by her husband...with everlasting love I will have pity on you" (Is. 54:1-8, LB). If you are a husband abandoned by a wife, God makes you the same promise. If the devil has you in a pity-party, kick the devil in the seat of his understanding, draw close to God, and God will draw close to you.

Psalm 68:5 is a strong promise for widows and single parents: God is "a father of the fatherless and a judge [defender] for the widows."

When my dad died, my mom and I lived several hundred miles apart. One day my mother's back went out, causing her to crumple to the kitchen floor. Lying there in intense pain, she cried out to God, "Jesus, You promised to be my righteous defense. You know I'm all alone and have no one to do all my housework. Please heal my back." Instantly she rose to her feet and hasn't had a twinge of back pain in seventeen years.

What He does for widows, He does for the fatherless or motherless. God offers the special power and comfort of His Fatherhood to the child or teen with only one parent. If you are a single parent, you need to keep a close relationship with Jesus Christ. He who "sticks closer than a brother" (Prov. 18:24) keeps His promises. Learn to follow Him.

No matter what your circumstances, remember:

> Eye has not seen, nor ear heard
> > Nor have entered into the heart of man
> The things which God has prepared for those who love Him.
>
> 1 Corinthians 2:9, NKJV

How to Stop Being Lonely

The devil's most powerful tactic against singles is loneliness, which leads to depression, even despair. Here are some steps you can take to win over loneliness.

1. Recognize the difference between being lonely and being alone. Anyone can profit from times alone — for prayer, study, work and so forth. But the Hebrew word in Genesis 2:18 commonly translated *alone* means "lonely": "It's not good for the man to be lonely." That's true for women too.

2. If you are lonely, admit it. Jesus Christ admitted His deepest emotions to His Father: "My soul is deeply grieved to the point of death" (Mark 14:34). Satan wants to wear you down (Dan. 7:25). Christ understands your loneliness at the deepest level. "Draw near with confidence" to your Lord (Heb. 4:16). If you need Christ-centered counseling, get it.

3. Counseling or not, get with God for directions. Develop a solid prayer life and spend time studying the Bible. A steady diet of TV and movies will not make you free. As you devour the Word of God, *Christ* will make you free (John 8:31-32).

4. Meet with other Christians. If you are an unmarried person of any age and lonely, "God sets the solitary in families" (Ps. 68:6, NKJV). Follow Jesus Christ out your door. Volunteer to baby-sit so a couple you love can have a night out. Don't turn down an invitation to fellowship with godly couples. Volunteer time to help campaign for a Christian politician. Get with a Christ-centered singles' group at the church to which God leads you. That will serve two purposes: (1) You can minister to them with His love, joy, peace and other fruit (Gal. 5:22-23), and (2) they can minister to you as well. Don't forsake assembling yourselves together (Heb. 10:25). Reach out and touch a lot of someones.

> What a wonderful God we have — he is the Father of our Lord Jesus Christ, the source of every mercy, and the one who so wonderfully comforts and strengthens us in our hardships and trials. And why does he do this? So that when others are troubled, needing our sympathy and encouragement, we can pass on to them this same help and comfort God has given us (2 Cor. 1:3-4, LB).

Do you really want the seven secrets of being happy? Bless somebody — and then do it six more times!

Until you are completely over depression, don't get too close to other depressed people. You'll depress each other all the more. Seek whole people who are genuinely happy in Christ. Get happy too.

5. Never allow yourself to wallow in self-pity. Self-pity comes from

Satan (Mark 8:33). Instead:

> Keep your eyes on Jesus, our leader and instructor. He was willing to die a shameful death on the cross because of the joy he knew would be his afterwards; and now he sits in the place of honor by the throne of God. If you want to keep from becoming fainthearted and weary, think about his patience as sinful men did such terrible things to him. After all, you have never yet struggled against sin and temptation until you sweat great drops of blood (Heb. 12:2-4, LB).
>
> ...Let us strip off anything that slows us down or holds us back, and especially those sins that wrap themselves so tightly around our feet and trip us up; and let us run with patience the particular race that God has set before us (Heb. 12:1, LB).

6. Don't allow yourself to worry about your age. Age is mind over matter. If you don't mind, it really doesn't matter.

7. Realize work is a blessing from God. Adam was given a job in paradise long before sin entered this world (Gen. 2:15). Never look at your job as a curse. Whatever job you have is your ministry assignment from the Lord. Eve was given the job of helping Adam (Gen. 2:18). Men and women are still being given jobs — as homemakers, doctors, teachers, scientists, mechanics, missionaries and so on.

8. Learn to relax, rest and have fun.

9. Exercise and get enough sleep.

10. Develop close friendships. You need a prayer partner of your own sex — one who will believe with you (Matt. 18:19), love and encourage you (1 Thess. 5:11; Heb. 3:13) and hold you accountable to God (Rom. 3:19) — and one for whom *you* can do the same. The relationship between David and Jonathan was godly in every way. In the same way, Ruth's love for her mother-in-law, Naomi, was godly. Ask the Lord to give you one or more close friends like these.

But I'm Told I Won't Be Complete Without Marriage

> See to it that no one takes you captive through philosophy and empty deception, according to the tradition of men, according to the elementary principles of the world, rather than according to Christ. For in Him all the fulness of Deity dwells in bodily form, and *in Him you have been made complete....* And let the peace of Christ rule in your hearts, to which indeed you were called in one body; and be thankful (Col. 2:8-10; 3:15, italics mine).

Two Witnesses for the Single Life

Two of my most valued friends are Bonnie Green and Marialice Smith. They are two glowing testimonies to the fulfilled life a single can live in Christ. Never married and approaching seventy years of age, these two ladies have spent their adult lives ministering together all over the world. Working with Teen Challenge and Youth With a Mission, they've led people to Jesus and strengthened Christians throughout the West Indies, the Caribbean and Europe and in Alaska and most of the continental United States. Living now in Leesburg, Florida, they still travel in ministry.

In answering why neither ever married, Bonnie says, "I was proposed to five times and engaged once. But I knew I could never love a man as I should if I were to marry. I felt as if they were brothers and women were sisters. It did bother me because I wasn't like the other girls who were getting married around me. It was all they thought about. In those days, if you didn't get married, most people figured there was something wrong with you. I believed that too. I had never heard Jesus Christ gives the gift of singleness."

Marialice says, "As a kid growing up, my parents wanted me to marry, and I supposed I would — sometime. As an adult I went from bookkeeping to designing parts for jet fighter planes. I was very proud of the money I made. I loved children and would have married to have them, but I didn't really want to marry. I dated a lot all through high school. I was proposed to twice and engaged twice. But I knew I didn't love any of those men."

Bonnie and Marialice didn't like each other when they met. Marialice thought Bonnie was spoiled, and Bonnie thought Marialice was jealous of her. However, two years later they became best friends after discussing their negative feelings for each other and giving those feelings to the Lord.

About being single for a lifetime, Marialice says, "The longer you stay single, the more selfish and narrow you become unless you completely give your life to Christ and your life is involved with others. You can have no self-pity because you're single."

Bonnie adds, "No one should fight their singleness. Instead pray, 'Whether it's for a season or for always, Lord, You always have my best in mind. I will accept my singleness and wait on You.' "

About sex, Bonnie laughs, "It's never been a problem since the moment I really surrendered my body to God as Romans 12:1-2 told me to do."

Marialice drives the point home: "It's sure not a problem with me either. Far more important, if either one of us had gotten married, we would have lost the joy of going wherever the wind of the Holy Spirit blows."

Two Nevers

Never marry and never go into a professional ministry as a career if you can do something else and be just as happy. If you can maintain a "take it or leave it" attitude with either of these lifetime commitments, you're not ready yet, or God isn't calling you to this purpose.

(1) Remember: Every Christian is engaged to Jesus Christ; as the church, we will celebrate our marriage to Him at "the marriage supper of the Lamb" (Rev. 19:9). (2) Full-time ministry should refer to any career or occupation you enter. If your life belongs to Jesus Christ, you will want to serve Him full-time at whatever you do best.

But What If I Still Want to Be Married?

Be anxious for nothing, but in everything by prayer and supplication with thanksgiving let your requests be made known to God. And the peace of God, which surpasses all comprehension, shall guard your hearts and your minds in Christ Jesus (Phil. 4:6-7).

Nothing that is within God's will is out of God's reach.

No singles' book concludes as well as Charles R. Swindoll's little booklet *Singleness*. I thank this great radio teacher and pastor for allowing me to end my book as he ended his:

Rejoice!

You do not need to wonder why you have missed the best. You *have* God's best. Since God is sovereignly in control, it's His call for you right now. It's not, "Some day when I'm married I will count for Christ." It is, "Since God has led me to be single, I will capitalize on the benefits that are mine to enjoy." Rejoice in the occasion that's provided for you.

Reverse!

Reverse the energy that you've been using up in the horizontal syndrome of panic and worry...and turn it to the vertical. You will be amazed at how good He is at finding you a mate *or* giving you satisfaction without a mate.

Relax!

Let's face it — a fellow is not going to be very interested in a woman who is sitting on the edge of her chair, biting her nails down to her knuckles, wondering when he's going to get with it. You tip your hand. And, fellows, God's still in the business of finding mates. Yours may not be in Africa or Spain; yours may be very close to you. But relax. Give all the controls of your life over to the Savior, my single friend. And as you relax, watch Him redirect your life toward others who could really use some things you have to offer.

My advice? Not "good luck," but rather **Rejoice! Reverse! Relax!** I dare you.

Dear heavenly Father:

Our confidence in You is strong and firm. We are thankful that our situation is no mystery to You. Calm our spirits with that thought. Show us how we can not only accept our single state, but flourish in it. There are unique difficulties we live with — misunderstandings, times of intense loneliness, distinct feelings of rejection, and very real temptations most people can't possibly imagine. But we are confident You will use even these troubles to mature our walk. We do desire to glorify Your name and to minister to others in an authentic and meaningful manner. Encourage us by opening doors of opportunity, then make us sensitive to You and bold in faith as we step through those doors to serve others who need what we can provide.

In the strong name of Christ, Amen.[1]

To keep your life in focus,
stay away from hocus-pocus,
and follow Jesus.

Questions for Reflection and Discussion

1. Answer the letter preceding this chapter. Should this person panic at forty?

2. For all Christians, "Christ Jesus...is our hope" (1 Tim. 1:1). Meditate on the following verses: Psalm 119:81-83; Jeremiah 17:7-8; Romans 4:18-21, 15:13; 1 Timothy 5:5; Hebrews 6:17-18; and 1 Peter 1:20-21. What is the place of hope in the life of a Christian? How would these verses apply to a single Christian who would like to be married but isn't? Write down your answers, then discuss them.

3. Review the ten steps given in this chapter on how to stop being lonely. What is the danger of not *actively* doing something about loneliness in your own life? Can loneliness ever play a positive role in your life? Discuss successful ways you or your friends have used to overcome loneliness. Do you notice any patterns? Discuss your answers.

4. Romans 8:28 is one of the most difficult verses for Christians to believe, and yet this verse is as true as any other. Notice this verse doesn't say that all things *are* good or that you will necessarily *feel* good at the time they happen. Many single Christians fail to see how their staying single can be used by God for good. But wouldn't this verse be true even if you never got married? Read the comments by Bonnie Green and Marialice Smith. Can you see the truth of this verse in their lives?

5. As a single believer, you are in fact "engaged to Jesus Christ" (Rev. 19:9), and your life-style should be a strong witness to others all the time. Why is it so important as a single Christian that you understand God has "a purpose and a hope" for your life (Jer. 29:11) and that He can use you only if you are willing? Does your desire for marriage override your desire to serve the Lord where you are right now in your life?

NOTES

Introduction: Getting the Right Start

1. Phil Pringle, *Faith* (Sydney, Australia: Pax Trading Ministries Pty Limited, 1991), p. 12.
2. Patrick W. Morley, *I Surrender: Submitting to God in the Details of Life* (Brentwood, Tenn.: Wolgemuth & Hyatt, 1990), pp. 2-3.
3. Ray Mossholder, *Marriage Plus* (Lake Mary, Fla.: Creation House, 1990), p. 187.

Chapter 1: The Gift of Being Single

1. Penelope J. Stokes, "The Puzzle — Singles in the Church," *Family Life Today* (October 1983), p. 27.
2. John Fischer and Lia Fuller O'Neill, *Single Person's Identity* (Palo Alto, Calif.: Discover Publishing, 1973), pp. 1-2.
3. Stokes, *The Puzzle*, p. 27.
4. Harold Ivan Smith, *Singles Ask* (Minneapolis, Minn.: Augsburg, 1988), pp. 16-17.
5. George Barna, "Marriage and Divorce Towards the Year 2000," *Single Adult Ministries Journal* (Colorado Springs, Colo.: January 1990), p. 3.
6. Michael Cavanaugh, *God's Call to the Single Adult* (Springdale, Pa.: Whitaker House, 1986), p. 24.
7. Alan Redpath, *The Royal Route to Heaven: Studies in First Corinthians* (Old Tappan, N.J.: Fleming H. Revell, 1960), p. 92.
8. Fischer and O'Neill, *Single Person's Identity*, p. 7.

Chapter 2: Becoming Whole

1. Larry Tomczak, *Straightforward: Why Wait Till Marriage?* (Plainfield, N.J.: Logos, 1978), p. 103.
2. Calvin Miller, *Becoming: Your Self in the Making* (Old Tappan, N.J.: Fleming H. Revell, 1987), pp. 82-83.

3. Rich Buhler, *Love, No Strings Attached* (Nashville, Tenn.: Thomas Nelson, 1987), pp. 137-138.

4. Melody Green, *But I Can't Forgive Myself* (Last Days Ministries, P.O. Box 40, Lindale, TX 75771-0040, 1985). All rights reserved.

5. Tomczak, *Straightforward*, p. 108.

Chapter 4: What About My Special Case?

1. Art Levine, "The Second Time Around: Realities of Remarriage," *U.S. News and World Report* (January 29, 1990), p. 50.

Chapter 5: How to Make Yourself Attractive to Others

1. William Arthur Ward, writer in residence at Texas Wesleyan University, Fort Worth, Texas, publication source unknown.

2. Robert Baron, professor at Rensselaer Polytechnic Institute, Troy, New York, publication source unknown.

3. Croft M. Pentz, *The Complete Book of Zingers* (Wheaton, Ill.: Tyndale House, 1990), pp. 113,116,114; ending one-liner, p. 115.

Chapter 7: Wrong Reasons for Getting Married

1. Nancy Martin, *Unplanned Pregnancy: Making Wise Choices* (Nancy Martin, P.O. Box 3315, Culver City, CA 90231), p. 14.

2. Josh McDowell and Paul Lewis, *Givers, Takers, and Other Kinds of Lovers* (Wheaton, Ill.: Tyndale House, 1980), pp. 52-53.

Chapter 8: What Is Real Love?

1. Ann Landers, *Love or Infatuation*. Permission granted by Ann Landers and Creators Syndicate.

2. "Parents Involved in Tragedy Meet and Pray," *The Marlborough Post* (November 8, 1977), p. 1

Chapter 9: The Engagement Arrangement

1. Michael Zadig, "Marriage: Who Needs It?," *HIS* (March 1977), p. 10. Used by permission of InterVarsity Press.

Chapter 10: How to Keep Your Sex Drive in Neutral

1. Ann Landers. Permission granted by Ann Landers and Creators Syndicate.

2. "U.S. Supreme Court Supports Ruling: 'Boyfriend Can't Sleep Over,' " *Single Adult Ministries Journal* (Colorado Springs, Colo., February 1990), p. 6.

3. "Minesota Landlord Fights Back," *Single Adult Ministries Journal* (Colorado Springs, Colo., December 1990), p. 2.

4. John Eldredge, "The AIDS Scare, 10 Years Later," *Focus on the Family: Citizen* (December 17, 1990), p. 13.

5. Joseph Carey, "Condoms May Not Stop AIDS," *U.S. News and World Report* (October 19, 1987), p. 83.

6. Tomczak, *Straightforward*, p. 56.

7. Winkie Pratney, *Youth Aflame* (Minneapolis, Minn.: Bethany House, 1983), pp. 120-121. Used by permission of the publisher.

8. Tape #2181, available from Soundword Tapes, Church on the Way, 14300 Sherman Way, Van Nuys, CA 91405.

9. Al Menconi, "Is TV Destroying Christianity?" *Media Update* (November-December 1986), p. 3.

10. Ted Koppel, quoted in " 'Nightline' Host Ted Koppel Challenges Students at Duke," *The Forerunner* (Gainesville, Fla.: Maranatha Christian Churches, Inc., July 1987), p. 2.

11. Al Menconi and Dave Hart, *Today's Music: A Window to Your Child's Soul* (Elgin, Ill.: David C. Cook Publishing, 1990), p. 24.

12. Charles Colson, "Pornography Destroys Lives," *USA Today* (October 20, 1989), p. 13. Copyright © 1989. Prison Fellowship. Reprinted with permission.

13. McDowell and Lewis, *Givers, Takers*, pp. 55-56.

14. Ibid, p. 56.

Chapter 11: What If I Never Get Married?

1. Charles Swindoll, *Singleness* (Portland, Ore.: Multnomah Press, 1981), pp. 23-24. Used by permission of the publisher.

I'd very much like to know what this book means to you. Please write or call.

For full information about live Singles Plus and Marriage Plus seminars or for a catalog of audio and video tapes of these seminars and other messages by Ray and Arlyne Mossholder, please write to:

MARRIAGE PLUS
P.O. Box 4105
Chatsworth, CA 91313
(818) 882-9424